Six and Eleven

A Television News Anchor's Story

Ed Dague

Six and Eleven

A Television News Anchor's Story

By Ed Dague

Three Lakes Publishing

Clifton Park, N. Y.

Library of Congress Control Number 2010939682

ISBN 9780984343010

Printed in the United States of America

To Josh, Tucker, Henry

And Charlie

Introduction

It took place about 15 years ago. I'd just left my job as managing editor of the Albany Times Union to become the newspaper's lead metro columnist. I was on camera in the Channel 13 studios on North Pearl Street. Ed Dague, the main anchor on Channel 13, was interviewing me about the new gig.

"We're doing the same thing," Dague said to me.

"Well," I said in response, "We're doing the same thing more or less. There are some dramatic differences between what television does and what print does, and I think that's good."

"People need both," Dague said. "We're fast; you're in depth. We don't have depth, and I give speeches all the time saying, 'Please read the paper or don't vote.'"

I said, "Well, the idea of the media is that we should compliment one another, and anybody who relies on any one of us individually is going to miss out on something."

Dague said to me, "Why do print guys have so much trouble understanding television -- or do they not want to? I sometimes feel there's a …uh … maybe some envy."

"Well, we try very hard to pretend that you don't exist," I said. "Doesn't that make sense?"

He was right, of course. Print journalists have always envied TV journalists both for their celebrity and for the speed with which they can get their reporting in front of the audience. Ed was also right that anybody who only watches and listens to the news instead of reading it as well ends up poorly informed – that a newspaper provides more detail and, generally, more sophisticated reporting even in this, a period of conspicuous decline for newspapers. What print too often does not provide is the visceral, emotional connection through which television news can connect people on a gut level with the world in which they live. In ways that print can't, TV news can make people care about what's going on around them, and they should care about it.

Nobody did that better than Ed Dague when he was on the air. He understood what his medium was good at and what it was not good at, and he spent a glowing career playing to TV's strengths in getting out the news.

That brief interview with Ed Dague, I decided later, was probably the best conversation that I'd ever had with any television journalist either on or off the air on the topic of news coverage. Clearly, this was a subject that Ed had thought about, had turned over in his mind and had analyzed in some depth. Moreover, it clearly was a topic that was important to him. I found myself very much impressed with the guy. I still am. That's why I'm writing the introduction to Ed's book.

If you think it's easy to sit in front of a TV camera and present the news on deadline with both clarity and verve, think again. Ed Dague did that for decades with 100,000 sets of eyeballs glued on him twice a day. If you think it's easy to whittle down all the day's events, weighing their proper value to the viewer and positioning them accordingly in the newscast – into only a few minutes of air time, really – you're dreaming. And if you think it's easy to be both thorough and even-handed in doing that as you gnaw away like a dog at the bone of truth, then you lack a proper appreciation for the immense complexities of the task.

What's most interesting about Ed Dague is not that he was trained as an electrical engineer instead of as a journalist, not that he performed his duties on air for so long in intense physical pain that was resolutely hidden from viewers, not that he overcame a trying childhood or that he's universally well regarded by everybody in the news business who has had any dealings with him – even the print guys, like me.

What's most interesting about Ed Dague is that even as he rubbed elbows with the mighty he never lost his instinctive compassion for those cursed by centuries of persecution on the basis of their ancestry or for those who just never seem to catch a break in life. He identifies with people who are up against it. He frets over the future of young lives rotting away in bad schools in bad neighborhoods amid the splendor of broader American prosperity. He broods that so many will never find their way from those shadows into the bright sunshine of this society.

So, what we have here is a memoir presented from a unique perspective – from the special vantage point that a television anchor has of public events, public people, public issues and of the familiar faces that so many people in this town see every day on television. Ed Dague pulls no punches in this book. He spent decades presenting the news dispassionately and fairly, but that never meant that he was merely a cipher without thoughts or opinions on what was happening and where it all was going. This is a perceptive and thorough examination of both journalism and the television business in the Albany metro area. It's also the story of a man much more complex and thoughtful than he ever permitted himself to reveal in his role as the objective deliveryman of the news.

Ed Dague wasn't just a television anchor. He was a journalist devoted to helping people better understand the world around them in all its perpetually dismaying imperfection. He continues that noble task in this book.

- Dan Lynch
October, 2010

Ed Dague

Chapter 1: September 11, 2001

By 11 o'clock on the morning of 9/11, the newsroom at WNYT-NewsChannel 13 in Albany was already preparing to cover local aspects of the horrific terrorist attack 230 miles to the south. The station's top managers, the general manager and the news director, were out of town. They would be unable to fly back to Albany for days. The executive producer and the managing editor, which was my managerial position, already had a live truck headed to the State Emergency Management Office located near the State University of New York campus on Albany's Washington Avenue. Another remote truck already was stationed at the Leo O'Brien Federal building near the Hudson River in downtown Albany.

At the station, I was coordinating our coverage and preparing to anchor a local news cut-in when the need became clear and the timing made such a cut-in appropriate. The network coverage from New York City was then continuous at that point. I was reluctant to interrupt it until the pace of the breaking stories from Manhattan and Washington slowed. At about noon, as we confirmed the closing of the Albany federal building and learned of plans to close the state capitol and possibly all state offices, I decided to break into the NBC programming with a quick summary of the local developments.

Before going on air, I conveyed to the production staff in the studio that what I was about to say was probably less important than how I would say it. My intention was to project an air of calm. My goal was to avoid making viewers anxious or even more emotional over the still transpiring events. As the day went on, I found my biggest challenge was in keeping my own emotions in check. No tears would be shed on air; no sense of anger or fear or even bewilderment would be displayed.

It was simply a huge story. One of my early suspicions was that hundreds or even thousands of injured survivors would overload downstate medical facilities and require authorities to transport some victims to upstate hospitals with trauma centers. That suspicion proved to be wrong, but our mobilization of live capabilities toward Albany's hospitals put us in position to cover the massive surge of local people intending to donate blood at the Red Cross

Center near the three largest Albany hospitals. We recently had acquired a truck with a camera attached to the mast, which we raised to facilitate microwave transmissions. The "mast cam" gave us impressive shots of the hundreds of area residents standing in a line that eventually wrapped around the blood donation center.

We also had dispatched a reporter and photographer to New York City, aware that they probably would not get into Manhattan but believing they could probably originate reports from New Jersey or another area with a view of Manhattan. Our competitors, I knew, had dispatched their main anchors to New York City. I considered that a big mistake. My opinion was that viewers would want to see the anchors in studio, where they could coordinate reports and play a larger role in setting a tone for the local broadcasts.

My co-anchor, Lydia Kulbida, lived much further from the station than I did. She arrived a couple of hours later. We split up the afternoon's on-air responsibilities until early evening, when we began our extended local newscast with both of us on set. By that time, we had a wealth of reports – from state emergency management officials, the Red Cross, from homes of concerned local people with deep personal connections to the tragedy downstate. We also had a wealth of taped comment from government officials involved at every level.

Much of the NBC coverage was packed with heavy emotional content. Both Lydia and I worked at not allowing that to affect our on air demeanor. In the end, I was very proud of our news staff. Our reporters and producers worked tirelessly throughout the day to deliver meaningful and sometimes very emotional news to our viewers. I've always thought that television was inherently better able to convey more emotion than other news media. Pictures have emotional content even without the addition of words or music. We did, I think in hindsight, overuse the video of the World Trade Center towers collapsing. On the other hand, so did most American broadcasters.

My most successful broadcast in connection with 911 came a few weeks after the day itself and on the Albany public broadcasting system station. I'd been contacted by WMHT-Channel 17, the PBS station, a few days after 911 about moderating a community forum dedicated to calming religious and ethnic tensions stemming from the attacks on New York and Washington.

WMHT brought together an impressive group of academics, law enforcement leaders and clerics in front of an audience drawn from the community for the two-hour program.

My role was to direct the conversation and occasionally put panel members on the spot with pointed questions. I've had a lifelong interest in studying history. That served me well on that broadcast. I could pull up dates like 732 AD (when Charles Martel defeated the Islamic invaders of Europe at Tours) from memory and also put some of my study of religions to good use. The program helped viewers understand the dynamics involved in considerable depth, I thought, and made a real contribution to the community.

But I was personally affected by the terrorist attack at a very deep level, I think. My whole conception of an advancing world culture that would unite humanity was shattered. Because religious beliefs were so central to the motivation and the reaction of America, my pessimism grew exponentially. It was particularly difficult for me to accept President Bush's immediate declaration of a day of prayer to follow the attack so closely. I've always been repulsed by jingoism.

I knew before I left home on the morning of the attack that a sort of despondency was building within me. I feared it would not diminish for a very long time. It was something I could never show publicly, but it contributed to my willingness to retire 18 months later.

While 911 was a uniquely difficult day for news people, the time pressures it imposed on news broadcasters were in no way unique. I'd learned all about that years before, in 1977, at another Albany television station.

The boss had been unhappy. Almost every night after the 11 O'clock news on WRGB-Channel 6 ended, news director Don Decker would call the show's producer to critique the broadcast that had just ended. On one night in 1977, he was particularly unhappy. Decker disapproved of the assignment given the lone night reporter, and producer Walter Fritz offered an inadequate defense of that assignment. So, on the spot, Decker fired him.

Actually, Fritz stayed on the staff but was ousted as a producer. In television news, the producer is the person in charge of the newscast. The director is the person in charge of the technical aspects of the newscast. The cameras, video tapes and film segments were all controlled by the director when the broadcast was underway. Meanwhile, the producer sat in the control room next to the director to make last minute decisions about show content and timing.

On that night in 1977, Decker had no other producer on staff to take over the job Fritz had just lost. So, Decker gave the assignment to me. It was unusual, to say the least, but it was just a temporary assignment, I was told. My belief is that Decker meant it to be temporary at the time but later felt no urgent need to hire a producer, so the job of producing the late news remained mine for years.

It meant I would begin my work day at about 3 O'clock in the afternoon. My first consideration was usually the evening assignment. On most nights, just one reporter was working, so I would study the list of possible night stories and decide which one (sometimes two) to assign to the reporter and photographer who made up the night crew. It was a complicated decision because the photographer also would have to edit the filmed stories from earlier in the day, which I would then include in the eleven o'clock newscast.

That meant I had to consider the photographer's availability to edit when dispatching the night crew to cover a story. If the story involved significant travel time – say, to Berkshire County to the east or to Cobleskill, well west of Albany -- then I would have to limit the number of stories from earlier in the day that I wanted re-cut for the late news. So, the issue of assigning the night reporter was tied to the quality and quantity of reports produced by the daytime crews. Also, there always was the "breaking news" consideration.

The story given the night reporter would frequently have to be abandoned, sometimes after filming of the story had begun, so the crew could be shifted to a late breaking story. That meant I was always hesitant to send my single night crew too far from the heart of the Capital Region. Sending them too far away would put them out of position to respond to an evening murder or robbery or big fire or any number of other events that could happen unexpectedly and which had to be covered. On many nights, perhaps more often than not, I was working under a "no overtime" order. That meant I could not call in another photographer or reporter if a big story broke.

The breaking news story need not be local to upset my plans. The 11 o'clock newscast was a summary of the day's world, national and local developments. A big breaking international event could require local reaction. That would mean that my initial plan for the night crew would have to be abandoned. Something like the Apollo 13 crisis or the Yom Kippur War could wipe-out local stories and force a late redeployment of my crew just as readily as would a big area fire or crime.

All those possibilities had to be considered every day in assigning the night crew. That may explain why Walter Fritz handed a boring and insignificant assignment to his reporter on the night he lost his producer position. I was never certain that the boss understood all that Fritz was considering the night that Decker fired Fritz. One of my biggest complaints about Decker's management was that his moods too profoundly affected his decisions. In time, I found that he always loved the Friday 11 O'clock newscast because his mood improved after consuming a couple of beers as the weekend began.

When the night reporter's story had been assigned, it meant I'd begun to formulate the late newscast's local content. It signaled that I'd made some preliminary decisions about which dayside reports would be included in the newscast and that I'd now moved on to consider the national and international news. All of the networks sent a closed feed to affiliate stations in late afternoon. It was generally a half hour of varied reports fed one after another with no anchor or introduction. The related scripts were sent by teletype to the affiliate newsrooms.

The NBC closed feed was called NPS, for News Program Service. ABC had the best title for their closed feed -- the ABC Daily Electronic Feed -- which made it the ABCDEF. The stories included were usually produced by local affiliate stations and fed to the network for consideration. If the network included the local report on the closed feed, the local reporter got national exposure and a small payment (about $75). Some items on the closed feed were produced by network news operations. The Gene Shalit movie reviews moved routinely on that closed feed, for example.

NBC sent their NPS reports at five o'clock in the afternoon, and I monitored their transmission in a small announcer booth. I timed their reports and wrote a summary in a notebook. The station usually kept the tape of the network broadcast for one week. That meant that sometimes a report from an affiliate would be used locally days after it had been sent by the network. Often, the network feed included dated material from network correspondents on the top stories of the day. So, a presidential news conference might be summarized by the NBC Chief White House correspondent on the Nightly News, the big network newscast, and also summarized by others for the NPS feed to give local stations the option of having a previously unseen report for their late news broadcast.

Once the NPS feed was recorded and logged, I had to devote my attention to the 6 O'clock news. That was an hour long local newscast which I co-anchored with Ernie Tetrault. Between 5:30, when the NPS closed feed ended, and 6 O'clock, I had to put on my makeup, read and edit the 6 O'clock script and get in position in the studio for the broadcast. The minute that newscast ended, I ran back to the tiny booth where I had monitored the NPS feed to log the Nightly News broadcast so I could use excerpts from it in my late newscast.

That meant it was 7:30 before I had all the ingredients for the late newscast on hand and could begin to lay out that broadcast. My first step was generally to cut down the local news reports produced by the day side reporters. Often, that involved dubbing their audio narratives to a reel-to-reel tape machine so I could cut and splice the tape so that unwanted or unneeded phrases and sentences were eliminated.

The 6 O'clock hour-long newscast could and usually did accommodate reports longer than two minutes but the actual news hole – that's the time available for news content -- in the late news was 13 ½ minutes. Generally, I could edit a two-minute piece from the 6 O'clock report to 50 seconds or less for the late news. Early in my tenure as late news producer, my editing skills caused me trouble.

WRGB's labor agreement with the announcers union included payments called "talent fees." If a reporter's voice was used on air, the reporter was paid $2. If the reporter's image, (as in a standup,) appeared on air, the reporter got $4. The dayside reportorial staff used to lobby me to use their pieces so they would be paid the talent fees. When I cut out a standup, I was costing a reporter four dollars. Some complained that I was purposely cheating them to save the company's money. That was never a consideration on my part, but some reporters remained convinced that I was intentionally costing them talent fees. Another issue related to my producing concerned me more than the silliness over talent fees.

My ability to see relationships between stories meant that I would often see ways to tie local reports to bigger national issues. So, I frequently used just the sound bites from local interviews and eliminated most or all of the reporter's narrative that was unrelated to the bigger picture. The result was that my late newscasts seemed to move much more quickly than traditional newscasts, which included more reporter pieces. The TV news consultants used to count stories in a newscast as a measure of the newscast's pacing, but they couldn't easily do that with my late news scripts. That's because stories became so entwined that the "story count" might be one even though pieces of five local reports were included.

Some staffers objected to the pace of my newscasts. The reporters claimed that the newscasts were so fast as to become incomprehensible. In particular, a very good reporter named Sharon Smith objected to the style and pace of my late newscasts and took her objections to the boss. She had some newsroom allies. That caused me to reconsider and to sometimes doubt my writing and layout practices, but the audience seemed to respond to my newscasts. As is usual in broadcasting, if the ratings stay healthy, management is happy, and the late news ratings were always healthy.

On most nights, I had a late news show rundown complete by 9 O'clock, which was when the director wanted it. The rundown back then was typed and is now computerized, but the content remains the same. The rundown is a listing of the reports, segments, and commercial breaks to be aired and the order of their airing. The rundown includes running times and total times and sets the page numbers, video-tapes, and filmed items for the newscast. Once I'd completed that, it was all downhill, in my mind.

From the rundown, I would produce a tape list; a listing of all video tapes including sources, and in-cues and out-cues for the tape editor in the back room. Then, I would produce a film list including times and cues and projector assignments ("A" rolls and "B" rolls) for the photographers. The last thing to be written was the script. I had to start that by 10 O'clock or I'd be hard pressed to finish by 11.

Scripts were written on six-part copy sets in three columns. The left column was just for video. The right column was for just audio, including the words to be read by the anchor, and the appropriate out-cues. The center column was for time and was the controlling item in most scripts. The "B" rolls were all aired according to the time column and the name identifiers for those interviewed -- called "supers" in TV, code for superimpositions – all were put up according to the time into the piece.

"B" roll films were simply videos aired to cover-up the video coming from the main report. That video was, of course, called the "A" roll. Sometimes, the "B" rolls covered jump cuts in the film editing. Sometimes, the "B" rolls were pictures of what the person on the "A" roll was talking about. They're gone from TV news today, since film is almost never used. The terminology remains, however. Sometimes today, a young reporter will tell a photographer to get "B" roll shots without having any idea where the term originated. It really goes back to the projectors used when film was the primary medium for TV news. There were even occasions when a reporter might want to dissolve from one scene to another as an interviewee describes the transition. That required the use of a third projector and was called, of course, a "C" roll.

If I could start writing the script for the late news by 10 O'clock, I was usually in good shape. I wanted to finish by 10:45 so I would have a few minutes to put on makeup, straighten my tie, and comb my hair before hitting the air at 10:58:56 with the late news tease. The newscast had to end exactly at 11:30 because Johnny Carson's Tonight Show was coming down the NBC Network line at exactly that time whether I was ready or not. If I was still reading the news, that was sloppy. If my news didn't fill all the time, that, too, was sloppy. It had to be dead-on every night.

With me both producing and anchoring, there was no one to sit on the control room next to the director to make timing adjustments. Generally, during a live newscast, too many stories are deliberately prepared for the time allotted. It is far easier to eliminate a page than to add one, and the timing must be exact. So, when producing and anchoring, I got into the habit of checking the clock every time I introduced an item. If the item started later than the rundown indicated it should have, I would tell the director in the control room to kill a following page.

In normal productions, the anchor listens to the producer's instruction in the earpiece, but when I was doing both jobs I listened to the director in my earpiece. Well, that is, I did that until the engineers union objected. The technicians felt an announcer should not be listening to the technical communications. So, in the end, my communication to the director was through one of the people behind a camera or through a telephone handset mounted beneath the anchor desk.

From the anchor desk, I also would give the control room the off times for the sports and weather segments. Then the director would pass time cues to the sports and weather anchors through the cameramen or the floor director, if there was one. The floor director was the crew leader of the people behind the cameras. The floor director was on hand to set up props, if needed, and to give visual time cues to the performers. But management often considered the position to be extraneous. In times of tight budgets, the position was usually the first to be eliminated.

If everything went as planned, the newscast would start and end on time with no adjustment needed. That rarely happened. So, in practice, I was constantly adjusting throughout the half hour. On most nights, two or three pages would be removed from the script during the newscast. If the commercial blocks were not completely sold, non-paying spots would be inserted. Those could be public service announcements or promotional announcements for upcoming shows. Generally, I would leave those non-paying spots in the rundown so that I could dump them on the run if the program was running long.

Sometimes, the sports or weather segments would run long. That could cause me timing problems that were difficult to handle because those segments aired late in the newscast when my options were limited. The biggest problem for me as producer was performers deliberately running long. Sports was a nightly worry, since there was always one more score the sports anchor wanted to report. Weather was tough because the performance was entirely ad-libbed and more difficult to time out exactly.

The worst dynamic I encountered was between a sports reporter named Yaffe Lombardo and weather reporter Tim Welch. By then, weather had been moved ahead of sports. When Welch went long with his weather segment, the time would have to come out of the sports segment. One night, Lombardo decided that Welch was running too long consistently and, in Lombardo's judgment, deliberately. The pair started arguing on set as I was trying to close out the newscast. The argument escalated and became physical. I addressed the camera at one end of the studio, telling the audience, "That's our report tonight. Thank you for joining us. The Tonight Show with Johnny Carson is next. Stay tuned, and we'll see you tomorrow." Meanwhile, as I delivered my closing, Welch and Lombardo were engaged in a fist fight at the other end of the studio.

The combined job of anchor and producer was too much. After a full year of it, I wanted the station to hire a real producer and give me some relief. While doing the two jobs, I could never take a lunch break or even relax for 20 minutes. Sometimes, when late breaking stories hit the wires after 11 O'clock, I would try to get them on air by killing scripted pages and ad-libbing around wire service copy. A few times, I simply couldn't finish it all by 11 O'clock. So, during the sports or weather segments, I would run upstairs to the newsroom to finish writing the bottom of the show.

I complained about the workload to no avail. I ended up doing the two jobs for over three years. Then, when General Electric announced it would sell WRGB, the managers decided to buy the place themselves and became consumed with the minutia involved in setting up a corporation and finding business partners. Don Decker became so involved in that process that he missed a deadline for extending my personal service contract. When he tried to pick up the station's option after the deadline, I refused to allow it unless he hired a producer and gave me some relief at 11.

He did. There was a news assistant I'd intentionally trained to replace me as producer of the newscast. Margaret Dore was intelligent and motivated, and I'd taught her everything I could. I knew she could handle the job. Decker hired her, and she was terrific. I went back to reporting, which was always my favorite job, and finally got to take a dinner hour. Maggie Dore quit WRGB shortly before I did as a divisive strike made the station a tough place for journalists to work. I ran into her years later while covering the New Hampshire primary election for WNYT. She was there as a producer for NBC Network News working in Washington, DC. Hooray for her.

Chapter Two: My Life So Far

On a very few occasions in my life, my whole consciousness has shifted to a frighteningly broader perspective, and the shift has startled and nearly panicked me. One example is a memorable afternoon in 1952.

I was effortlessly vaulting over a series of backyard neighborhood fences while heading home. A sort of slow motion appreciation of the abilities I possessed as an 8-year-old boy took over, and I watched my journey from the perspective of a far older person, fully understanding the fleeting nature of my physical skills. I knew with absolute certainty that I would remember the incident forever because it involved what seemed to be an instant of special mental clarity involving the perspective of time.

These few moments in my life, often insignificant in all respects save the mental perspective, became embedded in my memory in an especially stunning way. One of my earliest such recollections is of exploring the tennis court on which my father had just finished playing a game. He gave up playing tennis after World War II ended. That locates my strangely vivid memory to on or before my second birthday, August 31, 1945. My exact recollection is about suddenly understanding how learning to walk had expanded my world. It was too lucid a thought for a toddler, it seems now, and that's why it rattled me enough to be remembered so vividly.

There was another mental shock in my early childhood experiences that I eventually put out of my mind for decades. At the time it struck, it kept me awake, thinking, for many nights. It happened in the second grade at the St. Theresa Roman Catholic Elementary school in Buffalo, New York. It was 1950 or 1951. There was a routine reading exercise underway in which whomever Sister Mary Angela called on had to stand and read aloud until she chose another reader.

I'd just finished my turn reading. As I took my seat after having done especially well, I suddenly knew with total certainty what I would do later in life. I would read out loud. It wasn't a plan. There was no thought process involved at all. I just knew that my emotional lift following a good reading performance was going to become a routine life experience. I knew it with overwhelming certainty, but, I had no idea what it meant.

Who got paid to read out loud? As hard as I pondered the issue, I simply couldn't imagine any circumstance in which I could be gainfully employed simply to read out loud. It really bothered me for weeks because I'd experienced such a strong mental impression.

The incident was forgotten long before high school and played no role in any of my early thoughts about a career. Then, one night more than 50 years later, I found myself lying awake in bed thinking about getting up early to drive to the Lansingburgh section of Troy, New York, where I had an appointment to read out loud to a second grade class. Then I remembered lying awake in bed thinking about reading out loud in my own second grade class. The whole incident came back in a rush and left me deeply puzzled. At last, I knew who would pay me to read aloud

The memory returned to me late in my career. In retrospect, my career path was essentially accidental. My intent after graduating high school was to become an engineer -- as ordered. All my life, I'd been told, I was going to be an engineer. I hadn't questioned it. I hadn't even thought about what engineers do. In college, I realized that I was surrounded by people who very much wanted careers in engineering. I also understood that I lacked the motivation most of them displayed. I had no idea what I wanted to do.

I'd grown up in the area around Buffalo. My father was an industrial engineer and a manager at the Bethlehem Steel Company's Lackawanna plant, once the third largest steel plant in America. My father, James Otto Dague, had grown up in Columbus, Ohio. He received his degree at Ohio State and moved to Buffalo in 1940, after having been recruited by Bethlehem for its management training program. He met Elizabeth Catherine Kelly in 1941 in her home town of Buffalo, married her in 1942 and the two had their first son in 1943. That was me.

They had a huge fight that began at their wedding reception and continued until their divorce in the 1970s. I recall few times when my parents could have been described as a loving couple. Most of the time they were fighting. Sometimes the conflicts became very physical. My father always won the physical fights. There were times when my mother would go weeks without being seen in public because of her visible bruises. At other times, she was gone for weeks or months on end, usually retreating to her parents' home in Buffalo to escape the relentless war.

Religion kept them together. My father claimed to have spent his first two years of college in a Roman Catholic seminary studying to be a priest, although I doubt that was true. His upbringing was certainly steeped in Catholicism. His mother was a fervent believer. My strongest memory of her is the prediction she made about her death. When I was 4, she told me about a miracle at Fatima in which Christ's mother had appeared to three young children and had given them three predictions, which were written down and were in the hands of the Vatican. The last one was to be opened in 1960, she told me in 1947, and that I would be alive when that occurred but she would be dead. She was right, but she was wrong, in my opinion, to discuss her death with a 4-year-old grandson. It scared me.

She'd given birth to two sons. One, my uncle Edward J. Dague, was the family star, apparently. All my father's relatives in Columbus told me over the years about her cruelty toward her second son -- the fat one without the sparkling personality, my father. The single most insensitive comment I've ever heard was made by her as she and my father stood over the casket of her oldest son, Ed Dague, after he died of meningitis in 1937. Crushed by the loss of her clear favorite, she had said to my father, "Oh, Jim, why couldn't it have been you?"

The strong religious beliefs that my father took from his mother, along with his concern for appearances, surely kept him married to my mother through nearly 30 years of warfare. Early on, I saw a lot of hypocrisy in that. You can't beat your wife on Saturday night and then sit in church with your son on Sunday morning professing a belief in love and peace. My father was strongly opinionated and wouldn't even talk to my mother's family when I was growing up because, he explained to me, all Irish people were scum. The Irish were a bit better than colored people, in his view. Negroes were sub-human, he maintained, and medical science would prove that soon.

My mother seemed to have no strong bias against any group of people. I didn't discover her anti-Semitic biases until 1968, after I'd married Donna Levy, a Jew. My mother's first visit to our apartment after my marriage was a disaster. She objected to being served "dirty black Jewish" food when my wife offered her a bagel. I was shocked at the bigotry, but my mother's younger sister explained it to me decades later as a religious bias common to Irish Catholic families that my mother had known while growing up. My mother's parents had been born in Ireland, as were two of her four siblings.

My parents had four children. The first three were boys. I was named after my father's dead brother. Two and a half years later, the second son was born. He was named James Otto Dague Jr., and always disliked the "Junior" following his name. Their third and last son was named Laurence William. He became closer to me than any other family member. Maybe that was caused in part by my father's obvious disdain for Larry. My mother always attributed that to the fact that Larry was named after her father. With his red hair, Larry probably looked disturbingly Irish to my father.

Their last child, Judith Ann, was the only girl. They'd waited years to have her because Bethlehem Steel Company told my father to stop having kids. The Lackawanna plant general manager actually told my father that the company did not like managers to have large families. My parents had Judy after that GM had moved on. Eventually, the steel company told my father where to live, what car to drive and what clubs to join. He followed instructions.

I did not. My entire life might be viewed as a rebellion against everything my father believed. I would like to think that my ideals and convictions stem from thoughtful analysis, but I recognize the commonly held psychological notion about rebellion against authority being especially prevalent among children raised in Catholic homes with a domineering father. Something made me emerge from childhood with unusual anger about how this society functioned. Something made me more interested in social equality and history than any contemporary I knew. I'd like to believe it was more than merely reaction to my upbringing, but I can never be sure. Whatever caused it, there's no doubt that my interest in history, politics, government, society and religion was so serious that I was usually out of step with the people around me. I still am.

Hypocrisy certainly had a lot to do with my disappointments with our civilization. It first confronted me in religion. Roman Catholicism started to fall apart to me in high school. I'd attended Catholic elementary schools through sixth grade and had been an altar boy from fifth grade onward. Those were the days of the Latin mass, so a great deal of rote memorization of prayers in Latin was a prerequisite. I served at masses through 10th grade and was chosen to be one of the servers on the altar at the pastor's funeral service. That was a different type of service called a Solemn High Requiem Mass. The Bishop of Buffalo presided. It was interesting to watch, but not as interesting as the Holy Saturday service.

That involved some procedures which struck me even then as being a bit silly. The priest washed someone's feet. I don't recall whose feet; they might have been his own, actually. Then the priest went outside the building and rapped on the church door with the end of a long wooden staff that was topped by a crucifix. (Another altar boy took the occasion to yell, "Charge!" and was scolded.) The priest then lit the fire that would live on in a continuously burning candle for the following year. That was especially interesting because I knew the fire had to be started using flint, and I couldn't wait to see how that was done. My disappointment when the priest produced an ordinary cigarette lighter is something I still recall. I wanted to see something far more primitive, like Stone Age flints.

The two priests who handled most of the services on Sunday, Fathers Herron and Baumgarten, knew I was beginning to doubt church doctrine by the time I was in eighth grade but could not or did not satisfactorily answer my questions. Some they dismissed as the result of "circular reasoning." Others were just deemed "mysteries" and proclaimed to be unknowable. When I went away to college, I stopped going to religious services altogether.

One of my strongest memories of serving at Catholic masses is of pain. It was there, while kneeling on marble, that I first recall experiencing severe back pain. That was in my early teenage years, and my parents dismissed it as "growing pains". I also started to experience a significant amount of neck, jaw and wrist pain, but I didn't give it a lot of thought. In high school, I walked the mile to my home every day after school. I recall attributing my increasing back and leg pains to that walk and never sought medical help. The physical pain wasn't yet too bad, but I now know that I have a progressive disease and that the level of pain will increase steadily throughout my life.

A bigger problem I experienced while growing up became an adult world problem as well. It seems to be an increasingly pervasive difficulty in modern America. It's a distinct bias against intelligence and learning. The educational policies of the 1950s must have been based on some theory favoring homogenous grouping of pupils. Even within a single classroom, students were bunched together by perceived intelligence. We were seated according to grade performance in the Catholic elementary schools. Those in the first row were often derided as "brownnosers" or "teacher's pets." They often were bullied. I was always seated in the first row.

It got worse in junior and senior high school. My family moved out of the City of Buffalo to a suburb named Orchard Park in 1953. My parents put me in the local Catholic elementary school, which was run by the same order of nuns I'd had as teachers in Buffalo, the Sisters of Mercy. The school had no classes beyond sixth grade so, in 1955, I entered the Orchard Park public schools. There, classes were smaller, but the homogenous grouping of students continued.

In seventh grade, they put me in a middle group. I won the class public speaking contest and got high grades, so the following year I was bumped up to the top group of the eighth graders. I stayed with that class through high school and felt some strong resentment from other students. The school administration's decision to group junior and senior high school students by grade performance guaranteed a divided student body. I hated it. I also hated the politics I saw within the school faculty. One of the best teachers I encountered, Russell Reed in junior year English, was penalized for his union activity. That struck me as terribly unfair.

In eighth grade, international politics affected my education and my life. The Soviet Union launched the first artificial Earth satellite. America reacted as if Pearl Harbor had been bombed again. The nation was failing to produce enough scientists and engineers. Why can't Johnny do calculus? Are American kids stupid? Sputnik 1 went up on October 4, 1957. By March of 1958, 13 eighth graders in my school, including me, were going in before school began so the high school principal could teach us ninth-grade algebra.

The following year, we were bumped ahead a year in science. That sort of thing happened all over America. In fact, nearly 50 years later, when I interviewed Rensselaer Polytechnic Institute President Dr. Shirley Jackson, she pointed to the reaction to Sputnik as the reason she became a scientist. There is no doubt that millions of students were pushed into studying science or engineering by school administrators reacting to the nation's panic over the Soviet satellite. In my case, it did not change any plans. My father had always told me I was to be an engineer. In fact, by the time I'd reached high school, he was telling me that it was the only college study that he would fund.

Another 1957 event affected me as well. The civil rights battle in America became heated when the President federalized the Arkansas National Guard and forcibly integrated schools in Little Rock. The television news pictures coming out of the South conflicted with what I'd been told about America. I realized I did not know a single black person. My school and community were all white. That started to trouble me because I felt deliberately isolated and sheltered from black people.

Social concerns were becoming extremely important to me. My emerging opinions started conflicts at home. It was the first time I encountered my father's radical racist views. It stunned me when he condemned President Eisenhower for his decision to federalize the Arkansas National Guard. I started listening to the adults around me -- in school, in the neighborhood and even in the Boy Scouts, where the adult leaders made racist jokes and comments I would not have noted in previous years. I began reading newspapers and novels like "The Last Angry Man" and "All the King's Men." My parents used to complain that all I did was read.

I graduated high school in 1961 with a set of moderate honors. I was inducted into the National Honor Society, got a letter of commendation' from the National Merit Scholarship people and won New York State Regents and engineering scholarships. I worried because I had done no real thinking about my future and was simply doing what I was told. A friend, a fellow ham radio operator who'd graduated from my high school a year before, had gone to RPI in Troy and flunked out. He told me about the college radio station, WRPI. What he said about the radio station made it seem appealing. So, I applied there. It was the only college application I completed, and I had no back up plan if I'd been rejected.

The day after high school graduation, my family moved to Harrisburg, Pennsylvania. My father had been made general manager of a money-losing steel plant in Steelton, Pennsylvania. My parents bought a house in suburban Camp Hill because the Bethlehem steel company had told my father that he should live across the Susquehanna River from Harrisburg. They also told him what car to buy and what clubs to join. That summer before college was just awful. I knew no one. I was minding three younger siblings because my parents had another argument and my mother had left, as she had so many times while I was growing up. She returned to Buffalo and stayed for weeks until I called her for help while dealing with my sister Judy's first menstruation. My mother returned to Pennsylvania a few weeks before I went off to Troy and RPI.

My father turned the Steelton plant into a profit-making operation in less than a year and became Bethlehem Steel Company's rising star. So, after just three years in Steelton, he was named general manager of Bethlehem's Burns Harbor plant, which was being built in Northern Indiana. The family moved to Valparaiso, Indiana. But before leaving Pennsylvania, my father told me something that made a huge impression on me.

I was home on a break from college. He picked me up at the airport. On the ride home he told me he was having trouble with the steelworkers' union at the Steelton plant. He'd named a new general foreman in a rolling mill but told me that the United Steelworkers union felt strongly that another man was more qualified.

"Well, is he?" I asked

My father answered that the man the union wanted was black.

I said, "So?"

My father answered, "No goddamn nigger is going to be a general foreman in my steel plant."

That ended the conversation. It was the second outrageous thing I recall him saying about steel plants. When I was much younger, we'd driven through the city of Lackawanna on a steamy summer day when the air pollution from the steel plant was especially heavy.

"You know," I recall him telling me, "these people who live here don't know it, but this stuff is killing them."

Even at a young age, probably between 8 and 10 years old, I was horrified. His two very memorable comments undoubtedly did a lot to shape my opinions about corporate America. His racial comment in Pennsylvania disgusted me, but I did not start a battle over it. I just sat in silence for the rest of the ride home.

Our battle over racial views did finally occur, but not in Pennsylvania. In Indiana, during my summer college break, my father arranged for me to meet a Roman Catholic priest who was vice-president for student affairs at Notre Dame University. His name was Father Daniel O'Neal, and he came to dinner at my parent's house in Valparaiso. I drove to South Bend and toured the Notre Dame campus with him before heading to Valparaiso, which was about an hours drive away. O'Neal's assignment from my father, he told me, was to bring me back to Catholicism.

I liked Father O'Neal a great deal. We talked about religion all the way from South Bend to Valparaiso. His conclusion seemed to be that the nuns had destroyed my understanding of his faith, and it would take a lot of discussion to undo their damage. He wanted me to transfer to Notre Dame. We also talked about my deepening depression about capitalism, about America's phony values and the war in Vietnam. He made no progress on bringing me back to his church, but we enjoyed a marvelously interesting discussion and we got along famously.

When we arrived at the house, I knew immediately that my father had been drinking. That was always a fearful thing to me. He'd long been a drinker and a mean drunk, but his alcohol intake had risen sharply in Indiana. At dinner, he started ridiculing me, as usual, so I deliberately moved the discussion to talk of race relations. I wondered how the priest would handle my father's racist views. Within half an hour, Father O'Neal was ordered out of the house. I drove him back to South Bend, embarrassed and exasperated.

By then, John F. Kennedy had been assassinated, and Lyndon Johnson was engaged in a war that I thought was immoral and stupid. Depression was sapping my ability to concentrate on engineering. Pain and fatigue took over, and I withdrew from RPI in 1964, during my junior year's second term. I went back after a semester off and tried switching to management engineering, but that was worse than electrical engineering, so I took off another semester and went back to studying electrical engineering. The time off from school ended my student deferment. As a result, I was drafted in the summer of 1964.

My intention when I reported to the induction center in Chicago was to refuse to serve. One of my high school friends had moved to Canada to avoid military service, but that seemed wrong to me. It seemed to me to be more honorable to refuse the draft and burden America with having to imprison me. I wore a suit for my expected court appearance and took no change of clothes with me, as I'd been instructed to do, so I'm fairly certain that the sergeant in charge of my group knew my intent.

The army physical exam got in the way, however. They took X-rays of my back and neck because of my posture and declared me unfit for military service. They reclassified me 4-F. The military medics had found a congenital deformity at my fifth lumbar vertebrae. So did a family doctor weeks later in Valparaiso. At last, I had an explanation for the increasingly debilitating back pain I was experiencing. Unfortunately, all the MD's were wrong. As it turned out, the deformity they'd spotted was not congenital. It was instead the result of a rare disease called Ankylosing Spondylitis. It wouldn't be correctly diagnosed until 20 years later.

The final split with my father occurred over Thanksgiving break in what was my senior year in 1966. We disagreed about everything, and I finally told him I did not want a career in engineering but was thinking about broadcasting. He ended all support and tuition payments, and I returned to Troy for good. It did not completely end contact between us. I never returned to Indiana, but when my father was transferred to the home office in Bethlehem, Pennsylvania, I visited a few times. My mother eventually got over her animosity toward Jews and became friendly with my wife's parents.

My father, mother and sister eventually moved to Florida after my father's early retirement, but the war between them continued. They divorced right after Judy graduated high school. My mother moved back to Buffalo and eventually settled in with my sister's family in Florida. My father remarried, then divorced again, then remarried the same woman. They were both alcoholics. The last time I saw my father he was in a psychiatric hospital suffering from brain damage from too much alcohol consumption. Before that, he'd made a driving trip to the homes of all four of his children.

His disdain for what I was doing for a living then was clear. He once screamed at me that "no goddamn TV reporter is going to tell me anything." He did, however, take note of how people in Albany treated me. During his final car trip to visit his children, he spent just two days with each of his offspring. On one of his two days with me, I took him to downtown Albany to show him where I worked. At the time, a state commission was investigating the Corning administration in Albany. We dropped in on the hearing. Then, I took him across the street to see the New York State Capitol building.

He did mention after that visit to Albany that he believed he'd seen people react with respect toward me. He watched me anchor one television newscast. He wasn't impressed, he said. After his return to Florida, I talked to him on the telephone occasionally. When he was hospitalized, my wife and I flew down to Florida to try to help out, but couldn't. When he died of a heart attack (unusual for an alcoholic, I was told), all his papers came to me. One was a letter to him from the president of Bethlehem Steel confirming that he would receive an extra $12,000 yearly in his pension for remaining quiet about something. The letter didn't say what.

My father had been summoned to Chicago right after retirement to testify before a federal grand jury about kickbacks paid during the construction of Bethlehem's Burns Harbor plant. He was not indicted, but several of his assistants as well as his successor as general manager were charged. A close friend and colleague of his, Jack Roberts, whom he'd brought to Indiana from the Lackawanna plant, also escaped indictment. I knew Jack Roberts but never met his young son, John, who was only 2 when his parents moved to join my father at the Indiana operation. That little boy is now Chief Justice of the United States.

I had much more contact with my mother after moving to New York's Capital Region. She and my wife, Donna, eventually came to get along, although the memory of their initial encounter was tough to forget altogether. My mother did learn to like bagels, but we never went so far as to have her try lox. She died of a heart attack 10 years after my father died. I'm not certain that she ever fully understood that my fundamental job was in journalism. My mother always thought of my career as being closer to entertainment. She wasn't wrong. Sometimes, I, too, felt more like a song and dance man than a reporter. That was part of what drove television ratings and kept me employed. She never considered my work to be dishonorable, however, as my father seemed to view it.

Neither parent understood broadcasting. Neither followed my effort to establish a career in that business. I had gotten a Federal Communications

Commission first class radiotelephone license in 1965, and RPI had hired me to operate the college's AM station, WHAZ. The school wanted to sell the station but had to keep it on the air to retain the license, which it had obtained in 1922. It was easy to find a commercial radio job with my license with RPI's recommendation, so I started at WOKO in Albany in December of 1966.

Initially, I helped the station adjust the phase differences between their towers to bring their signal pattern into compliance with FCC requirements. I worked for Chief Engineer Charlie Heisler, who'd helped put WTEN-TV and WROW-AM on the air and who still had contacts there. He knew the television station was looking for technical help and put me in touch with WTEN's chief engineer Bill Orr, who hired me. So, I worked from 3:30 to 11:30 for WTEN as a technician. Then I drove to WOKO for an all-night on-air shift as a disc jockey. WTEN has a picture of me there from 1967 working on a year-in-review program. The picture was displayed at a 1980's staff reunion.

The program director at Albany's WPTR AM, which was one of the big rock and roll powers in the '60s, heard my WOKO work and offered me more money to move to WPTR as the all night disc jockey. I continued working at WTEN until the two jobs became too tiring, so I chose to continue the on-air work and drop the technical job. Then, when Robert F. Kennedy was shot in June of 1968, WPTR fired me for refusing to play music rather than report on the breaking news from California on RFK's condition. By then, WOKO had been sold and the new owners hired me to start up a news department.

That was the huge turning point in my life. I liked gathering and reporting news. At WPTR, I'd conducted an on air campaign against the Vietnam War. I'd concluded that support for the war was the result of ignorance and that accurate, objective information was crucial to changing minds. Quality journalism suddenly appeared to me to be essential to ending the war, improving race relations, even to electing smarter people than the bozos then holding office.

For the first time, I'd encountered something that seemed positive and worth doing. Television was far more powerful than radio, clearly, so I decided I wanted to work as a television reporter. Having witnessed the news operation at WTEN-Channel 10 from the inside and concluding that it was not very professional, I wanted to work with smarter people. That seemed to mean working at WRGB-Channel 6. So, I began a year-long campaign to get hired by Channel 6 in Schenectady, just west of Albany, or at least by its radio partner, WGY 810-AM.

I started on June 15, 1969. News Director (or as the then-station owner, General Electric, identified him, Manager-News) Don Decker hired me to take on WGY's big noon newscast and all of the afternoon newscasts. My immediate goal was to make the noon report entirely fresh -- no more rehash of newspaper stories, which had been the basis for all the morning newscasts, but all new, updated reports with interview clips and thoughtful ramifications expanding on previous reports. I found that I could see possible stories where other journalists didn't. There were implications and contradictions occurring to me all the time where other reporters saw nothing. It is a capacity I never lost and that helped me tremendously throughout my career. I sat next to the television assignment editor Larry Schwartz and learned a lot from him about television production, but we disagreed often about what stories deserved coverage.

Then, just a year after I started working radio, Schwartz had a falling out with Decker – a not-unusual event in that newsroom -- and I moved straight to the television assignment/producer desk. Suddenly, with no education in journalism or even a single college writing course, I was in charge of the number one newscast's content, style, production and writing. It was an enormous leap for which I felt utterly unqualified. But I learned by watching the competitors and the networks, and I began trying new things regularly.

Because of the ailment that had saved me from the draft, I was in a lot of pain some days. I knew it affected my demeanor. Sometimes my back hurt so much by the end of the day that I wanted to scream, especially when the deadlines became terrifying. I was usually angry about the level of staffing. I knew the profit being made meant that GE simply was not returning enough to the community. I didn't like the conservative aura that came with corporate control, although I stifled real criticism of the existing power structure. I frequently objected to Decker's view of TV news, which -- to my mind -- ignored the visual potential of the medium in favor of talking heads. His treatment of the staff upset me greatly. That was what finally caused me to quit the station. But before that, I quit as assignment editor.

I wanted to report. It seemed impossible to quit as producer without quitting the station, but I did it. The best years of my career were the years covering the street as a reporter, roughly 1972 to 1977. The business was changing rapidly because of technical innovations. I experimented with all sorts of new techniques. Stand-up bridges meant the story had to take form on the road and not at a typewriter later. Natural sound was easier to capture and challenging to use properly. My work in Albany politics pushed me into a sort of beat there.

I revised the station's entire approach to election night. I took over a weekly high school quiz show and worked to enliven it. I developed an exclusive exit poll with RPI's management department, sped up the pace of the 11 O'clock news greatly by changing its basic concept and even designed the station's newsroom. When the news operation outgrew the small side office and moved to a much more roomy, but oddly divided room, the operations manager asked for help, so I drew the plan that he told me he ultimately adopted.

It was me who completely remodeled the contract between the company and the announcer's union, and I took over the Sunday morning interview program. I spent 15 years at WRGB and had an enormous impact on many aspects of the news operation. Then, in 1984, exactly 15 years to the day after I started working for WRGB, I quit and went across the street.

I'd almost left eight years before to take a network job. The NBC talent scout was a man named Bill Slatter. He'd sent one WRGB anchor, Don Craig, to Lebanon. In 1977, he approached me about moving to London for the network. I learned a lot just talking to Slatter. For example, I had a liability in that I was married and the network did not send married correspondents anywhere except London or Paris. The London bureau was responsible for all the British Isles and all of Africa, with the exception of the Middle East. The Paris bureau covered all of Europe, in theory.

NBC thought families could accompany correspondents to London or Paris but nowhere else. All married overseas correspondents who were sent elsewhere, Slatter told me, ended up eventually divorced. The network didn't give a damn about marriages, he told me, but the money and time lost flying people back to America for custody hearings, support disputes and divorce proceedings convinced the bosses that married men were too expensive. I prepared a tape for him. My favorite cameraman, Kenny Comstock, shot the narrative stand-ups for the resume tape in the woods behind my house.

Slatter called a month after I sent it and told me that three of the four managers who had to approve my hiring had viewed and liked my tape, but the last guy would never see it. Instead of hiring, the economy dictated that NBC was going to be laying off people, he said. My foreign correspondent job disappeared, but Slatter told me that he was empowered to offer me a reporter job at any network owned-and-operated station that I might choose. Those were the big NBC stations in New York City, Los Angles, Chicago, etc. I declined his offer because there was no big city in which I wanted to raise my kids (except London or Paris, maybe). He was disappointed and stayed in yearly contact.

The most interesting aspect of his continuing friendship was the call he made to WRGB in 1984, two days after I'd quit. All he wanted was my home telephone number, but the people in the Channel 6 newsroom, who had no idea where I was headed, were set buzzing by his call. In fact, he was coming to town and wanted to have dinner and talk. I took him to Lombardo's restaurant in downtown Albany, and he was wowed by the place.

In fact, I was committed to move to WNYT before he called. He thought that was a bad idea.

"It rarely works out," he told me, meaning that an anchorman quitting a station and going to a competitor rarely causes a big ratings boost. He thought I was taking a big chance, and I agreed. In fact, before I signed with WNYT, they got spooked and become unsure about our agreement. Neither of us had expected the storm that WRGB created over my move. So, I then agreed to have dinner with the WTEN-Channel 10 general manager, Ron Polera, who wanted me to co-anchor with that station's then-anchor, Dick Wood. I like Wood a lot, but I had no interest in merely anchoring anywhere. I had ideas about newscast content and format that I wanted to put into action. My best chance to do that was at WNYT-Channel 13.

Things got tense after I'd been off air at WRGB for about three weeks. The general manager of WRGB finally had his lawyer call my lawyer to inform him that Channel 6 was about to put out a press release saying that I'd suffered a nervous breakdown. My lawyer, Carl Engstrom, answered brilliantly.

He said, "Ed has written a statement of his own detailing the role of certain female managers at WRGB. I tell you what. You release your statement, and I'll release Ed's and we'll see what happens."

Within a half hour, the WRGB lawyer called again. Now he wanted to make a deal to settle the dispute. I started working at WNYT the following week.

Did I really prepare a press release about a key WRGB executive giving a job to a woman suspected by some of being his girlfriend? No. Did my lawyer really have my permission to release information about that woman's role at WRGB? No. But it was a great bluff by my lawyer, and it worked. It made me suspect that the rumored hanky-panky at WRGB might have had some truth behind it.

I started working at WNYT in July of 1984. I spent 19 years at the station, all of them better than any single year at WRGB. I worked with news director Steve Baboulis, whom I'd met years earlier, and with general manager Don Perry, whom I'd met for the first time two months earlier. It was not all sweet and happy at WNYT. We did have disagreements and struggles, but I always had more respect for Baboulis and Perry than I did for the managers at WRGB.

One of the first things I did at WNYT was to attend the station's annual picnic. I pitched most of a softball game and had a good time. Two days later, my knees were very swollen, and my back hurt so much I could hardly walk or sit. I went to my family doctor in Schenectady, Marvin Humphrey. He examined me in his office and took no radiographs. He told me, "You have Marie-Strumpell's disease," and sent me to the chief of rheumatology at the Albany Medical Center.

That amazed the doctors and professors at the Albany Medical College. They couldn't believe that a general practice physician working without pictures, blood tests or much else could diagnose a disease as rare as the one first identified by Doctors Marie and Strumpell. It's a disease now called Ankylosing Spondylitis. It's a progressive form of rheumatoid arthritis that affects most of my joints, but especially my back and neck. It is very painful, at times.

On the night of February 13, 2003, I was in so much pain on set that I moved across the studio to a more comfortable chair during the weather report. My co-anchor, Lydia Kulbida, came over and started to massage my shoulder, but any touch was so painful that I nearly screamed. That's why she and I both claim that my career was ended by an assault by my co-anchor.

My doctors had first suggested I retire three years previously. When I saw the rheumatologist the following morning, he again said that I was causing damage to my body by anchoring and should retire. I took his advice, and I wish I had done so earlier. My pain diminished upon retirement. My continuing concern now is that I've been taking methadone for pain for years and know the drug is highly addictive. That means I'll be taking it forever, or until I die, whichever comes first.

Chapter Three: The Mayor and Me

The tip was from a solid source but was proving difficult to confirm. At least two Albany police officers, my tipster told me, had been arrested the previous evening after being caught breaking into a truck parked behind a warehouse in the city. It was the early autumn of 1968, and such news in Albany was still controlled by a powerful political organization, known as the O'Connell-Corning Machine. It had held power in the city for nearly 50 years. Confirmation of news as big as a case of police corruption in the city usually could come only with the approval one of the named political bosses.

O'Connell at that time meant Daniel P. O'Connell, the curmudgeonly brother of the organization's primary founder and, by 1968, a reclusive old man. Corning now meant Erastus Corning 2nd, mayor of Albany and the scion of the aristocratic family that had helped the O'Connell brothers dislodge a corrupt GOP organization in the 1920s. Corning was a smooth-talking, immensely charming Yale graduate famous for finessing reporters with evasive or misleading answers. His secretary had already told me that the Mayor knew nothing about supposedly arrested police officers.

News reporting was new to me. I'd been at it officially for about three months after WOKO, a 5,000-watt AM radio station toward the top of the dial at 1400 KHz[1], had hired me as news director on the strength of an audition tape of a broadcast hagiography of Dr. Martin Luther King that I'd produced the night he was assassinated. It's likely that I'd spoken to Mayor Corning several times before that night in 1968, but no conversation before the police scandal story was significant. My memory of my relationship with Corning begins with the arrested cops incident.

Late in the day, the Republican candidate for Albany County district attorney called to notify me of a news conference he was calling for the morning. I feared he knew the police scandal details and that I'd been beaten on the

[1] Radio wave propagation diminishes as frequency increases. Stations low on the AM band were stronger for any given power than top of band stations at the same power.

story. The candidate was a shrewd suburban lawyer named Arnold Proskin. I pressed him repeatedly to give me a good reason to cover his event. He finally admitted that he had no announcement or revelation to make in the morning. It was just a matter, he told me, of two weeks having passed since his last press conference, and it seemed to be time for another. I concluded that he knew nothing about arrested cops. So, now more determined to confirm the police arrest story before being scooped by someone else, I came up with an idea.

I called the Albany mayor's office again and told his gatekeeper that I wanted to talk about Arnold Proskin's plans, which I figured would get me through to the mayor himself. When Corning said "Hello," I introduced myself as a reporter and told him that Arnold Proskin had just called a morning news conference.

I said, "I don't know for sure that Proskin knows about the arrested cops, but it seems to me to be better for you if I break this story on my tiny radio station than if Proskin breaks it as huge news tomorrow morning."

Erastus Corning 2nd replied, "I'll get right back to you."

Corning did not get back to me. Instead, I heard from Chief of Police Edward C. McArdle who called with the names of the arrested officers, the charges against them, and even their badge numbers. I broke it on WOKO's 5 O'clock newscast. The wire services picked it up and credited the station, which pleased my bosses. Before my next newscast, I called the area's biggest broadcast news operation to introduce myself by alerting them to the breaking story. It was the start of my campaign to get hired by WGY-850 AM-WRGB, a big TV-radio combo in the Albany metro area.

Arnold Proskin stunned the O'Connell-Corning machine by winning the election for district attorney in a county with a 2-1 Democratic enrollment edge. Maybe the story about the arrested police officers had some impact on the outcome. It probably would have become public without my work, but the political organization was reflexively secretive and the machine's cronies might have found a way to bury it. The public's perception of political cronies holding public office became a big issue in the 1968 election campaign. The Albany County Democratic party also lost its state legislative seats in a sweeping repudiation by voters. It looked like the end of the old machine. It was not.

Instead, it marked the emergence of Erastus Corning 2nd as the organization's real leader. He found that he could use the broadcast media to get around the local Hearst newspapers and gain direct and personal access to the public. Corning became a television personality through a series of weekly news conferences in which he demonstrated a spectacular ability to deflect any journalist's question, no matter how pointed it might be. It was entertaining political theater, and Erastus Corning was the unflappable star.

There was a story told I was told by several print reporters assigned to cover the state Capitol. It concerned criticism of the local press corps by R. W. Apple, Jr., a Pulitzer-prize winning New York Times reporter/editor who bet the local reporters a steak dinner that he could get a straight answer out of Corning where they could not. The locals took the bet and tipped off Corning, according to the story. At the next weekly news conference, Apple showed up but asked nothing until the meeting was nearly over. Then, he sprang his unavoidable query on Corning.

"Mr. Mayor," Apple began, "What is your favorite color?"

Corning replied, "Plaid."

It could have happened, I think. Corning 2nd was smart and educated and possessed a very quick wit. He'd graduated from both Yale and Groton Prep School, had formed his own successful insurance company to harvest the proceeds of his political clout and had become a real force in state politics. He'd devised a scheme to finance the construction of the billion-dollar Empire State Plaza in the heart of his city after Governor Nelson Rockefeller had concluded that a statewide bond proposal to build the Plaza would surely fail. Corning financed the project through the sale of Albany County bonds supported by the state's rent payments for the Plaza. His insurance firm, which had been the sole bidder on Albany County contracts for years, was also a beneficiary of contracts related to the Plaza.

My contact with Corning was limited during the remainder of my days working radio news, even after I moved to WGY-850 AM in June of 1969. But, to my total amazement, I became WRGB's assignment editor and main newscast producer barely a year after that. That put me in charge of reporter's daily assignments and, therefore, in charge of the content of the main newscast, which was then the 6 O'clock half-hour. In that job, I may have played a bigger role in Corning's emergence from Dan O'Connell's shadow in the public's mind than I realized at the time. It happened on O'Connell's 85th birthday, November 13, 1970.

O'Connell was a mysterious figure to most people in Albany at the time. He was almost never seen in public, and his personality was shrouded by the inscrutability of secretive power. As far as I knew, the last journalist to have actually interviewed O'Connell did so on January 1, 1948. That reporter was Albany Times Union political writer Leo W. O'Brien. He later told me that his story describing O'Connell's endorsement of President Harry Truman for re-election was read in the White House. The story so pleased Truman that O'Connell was given control over all federal patronage in New York State following the President's re-election. O'Connell was so delighted with that outcome that he saw to it that the reporter was elected to Congress. O'Connell had that much power.

So, when I called O'Connell's house on his birthday, I had little hope of getting anywhere, but a political friend had told me that O'Connell watched WRGB's news because he liked anchorman Ernie Tetrault. So, that was where I began my approach.

I called and said, "Hello, Mr. O'Connell and Happy Birthday. My name is Ed Dague, and I'm a reporter for WRGB -- Ernie Tetrault's station."

"I like Ernie," was the raspy reply.

"I would like to send Ernie to meet you," I said, "to interview you. Would that be all right?"

"Yeah, someday," I recall him saying.

I then pressed. I said, "I'd like to send him today."

"No, not today, but someday," said Boss O'Connell.

I wished him well and said goodbye. Then I called Ernie Tetrault at home and told him: "You aren't going to believe this, but I've got an interview set for you with Dan O'Connell at his house. I've got Roy gearing up to leave as soon as you can get to the station."

Tetrault got to O'Connell's house just after 2:30 that afternoon. He told me later, while laughing at what I had done, that he'd gone to O'Connell's back door carrying lights and the tripod and had been received warmly and invited right in. I really didn't think that I'd taken a very big chance. A good part of journalism is about sizing people up, and I read Dan O'Connell as a person who would never rudely turn away someone he knew and liked. Tetrault was very pleased, since he'd just gotten the biggest scoop of the year.

Alas, we were still shooting film in 1970, and film had to be developed before it could be aired. Tetrault got back to the station in Schenectady after 5 PM, so I finally got developed film after the 6 O'clock newscast was on the air. I could cut just one clip of O'Connell. The clip would have no real content and would run dead last. It was a 10-second tease that began with Tetrault talking off camera.

"Happy Birthday, Mr. O'Connell," Tetrault said.

"Thanks, Ernie," O'Connell responded.

I wrote a script and sent it down to the studio. Then I finally made it to the control room, where I was supposed to have been all through the show. My script began: "Finally, tonight, Dan O'Connell has long been something of an enigma to the people of Albany..." I was demolished minutes later when I found that I had thrown the anchorman a huge curve. Tetrault was tired and when reading cold copy could not pronounce the word. 'enigma'.

It took me over a week to produce a multi-part series based on Tetrault's interview. When it aired, I think it diminished O'Connell by making it obvious that he was no longer physically capable of running the political organization. It raised Corning's perceived importance in the process or, as I saw it, it revealed the actual power structure behind the Democratic organization.

It had another effect that Erastus Corning asked me to counter years later. My assessment of O'Connell's inherent courtesy to people he found agreeable was correct, and it became obvious to every reporter in town that O'Connell would not brusquely turn anyone away. So, he became plagued by journalists knocking on his door. The mayor called me in the newsroom one day years later after a WTEN-Channel 10 gadfly reporter, Herb Starr, had made a fool both of himself and O'Connell with a stunningly inept interview. Corning, I found, really loved Dan O'Connell and wanted to shield the old man from the constant badgering. I understood Corning's motive but could do nothing to help him.

His disdain for Starr was always visible. When the reporter introduced himself to Corning by saying, "I'm Herb Starr from WTEN. That's spelled with two 'Rs', Corning observed "That's a damned odd way to spell Herb."

One day, I watched Starr extol his previous night's reporting to Corning, which drew the response, "Well, Herb, I guess even you can't lose them all." Then there was the time I thought I had Corning set-up for a killer question after getting three preliminary answers. As I started to ask that question, though, Starr interrupted with, "Mayor, why do you always wear green socks?" Corning smiled at me, knowing that he had dodged my bullet and then answered the green sock question. It is understandable that Corning wanted to spare his old friend from encounters with Starr.

When the aged O'Connell died in 1977, Corning became County Democratic chairman in name as well as in practice. By then, Corning had gotten through his most challenging period in office. His administration had been besieged by critics and investigations throughout the early 1970s.

When Albany's population fell below a New York constitutional threshold number in the 1970 census, an elected school board became a likelihood. Corning preferred to name the school board members himself. In response to the census problem, Corning publicly asked Governor Nelson Rockefeller to veto the enabling state legislation. When Rockefeller vacillated, Corning used his grip on county government to disrupt financing for the governor's massive downtown building project. Albany County Attorney John Clyne halted the sale of county bonds for the project until Rockefeller announced his veto of the Albany school board bill. Bond sales then resumed, construction continued and Erastus Corning appointed the school board members for another year. The mayor had demonstrated to everyone that he had put Rockefeller in an impossible bind.

A taxpayers association was formed by an intelligent and dogged woman named Theresa Cooke. Simultaneously, prominent and wealthy Albany businessman Carl Touhey launched a professional campaign contesting Corning's reelection. The mayor fended off both challengers. Within a decade, his organization had won back all of the public offices lost in the 1968 election debacle. As a television reporter after 1971, I covered it all and began drawing attention because of my tough questioning of Corning. I would prepare for his press conferences for hours, thinking and rethinking about ways to pose important questions so he couldn't evade the issues. Despite years of effort by me, only once did I see Corning flinch.

During the early 1970s, anti-war protests and civil rights demonstrations riled America and raised tensions in Albany. African-American students in Albany High School seized the school auditorium and began a sit-in as a protest against perceived racism. The local NAACP leader, a State University of New York at Albany professor named Dr. Harry Hamilton, entered the auditorium and claimed to have negotiated a peaceful end to the incident. Unfortunately, the Hamilton agreement was reached too late. The city police SWAT team had stormed the room. It was a violent end to the event that had apparently been unnecessary. The following morning, I stood with a group of reporters outside Albany City Hall waiting to ambush Corning on his way into the building. He argued in support of the police action, called the situation potentially explosive and insisted that the police had no way of knowing that Dr. Hamilton had brokered an end to the event. My instantaneous follow-up question was, "Did they ask?"

His head snapped back, and he started looking at other reporters, hoping for another question. None came so he looked back at me and almost mumbled, "I don't know." He was rattled. It was the first and only time I was able to do that with Corning. It wasn't an especially difficult question to handle. I'd asked many that were far harder -- so many that he might have considered me an enemy. He did not. Years later, as Corning lay near death in a hospital room, he gave me an exclusive interview. I asked him why my habitually tough questions had not alienated him. He said, "Because the questions were always fair." We also had some common interests that played a surprising role in triggering a closer bond.

In the city hall foyer, he mentioned idly one day that his wife was throwing a birthday party for him. I asked him his birth date.

"October seventh," he replied.

I said, "Certainly a significant day in history."

Corning responded by saying, "You know, I've always wanted to write a book about the role of the Irish in the American Revolutionary War."

I said, "You're talking about Timothy Murphy."

Corning seemed surprised that I'd known about Tim Murphy. He then told me, "Young man, we should talk." The conversation marked a change in our relationship. Corning was an avid history buff. As it turned out, he and I shared a special interest in the Battle of Saratoga, fought just north of Albany in 1777.

A few years later, we finally did talk about the most important historical event that ever occurred along the Hudson River. Corning had arranged for an office stopover by an enormous copper kettle. He wanted me to see it because the kettle had once belonged to the invading British army of General John Burgoyne. The kettle was on its way to the nearby New York State Museum, but Corning had borrowed it for a few days. An open vessel clearly intended to be suspended above a fire, it must have been nearly four feet in diameter at the top. He did all the talking, and there's no doubt that he knew a great deal more about the battle than I did.

On October 7, 1777, as British General Simon Fraser tried to regroup his shaken grenadiers at Bemis Heights on the Hudson's western shore, Lt. Colonel Daniel Morgan of Virginia gathered five of his best marksmen, pointed across the battlefield at Fraser and reportedly said: "That gallant officer on horseback is a man I deeply respect. But it is necessary that he die today." History says one of Morgan's riflemen, Timothy Murphy, climbed a nearby tree, fired and mortally wounded Fraser. When Fraser fell, Morgan ordered his men to charge. The vaunted British grenadiers broke and ran, exposing Burgoyne's entire flank. The rout was on, and the Battle of Saratoga was won by the rebels. It all had happened on what later became Corning's birthday.

It is easy to talk to someone, anyone, about his or her birthday. The death day is a far more difficult topic to broach. But, after O'Connell's death in 1977, we at WRGB-Channel 6 News in Albany realized we had to prepare an obituary for Corning so we could effectively cover a sudden and unexpected death. I was assigned that task. It was a difficult one because Corning's life story was essentially unknown even though he'd sprung from a prominent Albany family. I needed Corning's help in putting together the report, but how do you ask a man to help you write his obituary? Finally, I found a time and place. On Labor Day in 1982, Corning came to the WRGB studios to appear on one of the Jerry Lewis telethon local segments. During a break, I went to the men's room and found myself at a urinal next to the mayor.

"This is the place," I announced to him.

"The place for what?" he asked.

I explained that I'd been thinking for months about how to ask him for help. As we were both responding to the call of nature, it seemed appropriate to bring up another part of nature -- death. He laughed and said he would be happy to help. So, weeks later, I sat in his office for a one hour long frank discussion of his life. One absolute rule governed the discussion. I would use nothing learned there until after Corning had passed away.

I began by asking about his family. I knew that he had two children and that his daughter, Bettina, lived in Philadelphia, his wife's home town. When I asked where his son was then living, Corning said sadly, "I don't know. He's somewhere between Moscow and Hawaii. We're not very close. I wasn't a very good father to him."

Corning explained that he'd been busy running for office when his son was young. Then the mayor had gone off for service in World War II and, "By the time I came back from the war, he was in boarding school, so I never really got to know him."

This discussion was very frank. I even asked about his wife Elizabeth and about his assumed mistress, a prominent fixture of Albany County politics named Polly Noonan. (Of course, I never used the word mistress.). Elizabeth and he had few common interests, Corning told me. His wife was interested in flowers and gardens and society, all of which he found dull. I did not ask – nor did he volunteer -- any information about whether his relationship with Polly was ever physical. He did tell me, however, that when Polly first showed up at city hall with a job given her by Dan O'Connell, Corning had believed that O'Connell had put her there to spy on him. So, as Corning routinely did with so many other potential political enemies, the mayor had used his charm to co-opt her and turn her into his ally.

I also questioned him about his apparent total involvement in every aspect of city business. I wondered why he seemed to make every decision, no matter how small, as we'd so frequently heard from every city department head. And I asked why he'd never left Albany, since I believed he'd been offered a position in the Kennedy administration. He had been offered such a job, he told me, but the position in question had been well below cabinet level and not very interesting to Corning. Besides, he said, he was very comfortable in Albany and didn't want to be a small fish in somebody else's big pond.

I heard some fascinating things in that session with the mayor -- such as the story of his last cockfight. He used to attend the highly illegal cockfights with his Uncle Parker and Dan O'Connell in the 1930s. Then, one night, while sitting there next to O'Connell, Dan turned to Corning and told him, "This is your last cockfight."

"Why?" Corning told me he asked O'Connell. Corning received the answer that he was running for mayor and that a mayor cannot attend a cockfight.

"Why not?" Corning said. " I'm a state senator now."

Corning told me he then got an answer from O'Connell that I can only paraphrase. A mayor can't attend a cockfight because he has to be respected, O'Connell explained. But, a state senator can attend cockfights because nobody expects much of him anyway.

Corning also loaned me a book from his private library after warning me to take great care of it. It was about an earlier Erastus Corning, great-grandfather of the mayor, and it was an inspiring story. Crippled as an infant in a collapsing crib accident, the first Erastus Corning had moved from Connecticut to Troy, New York, at age 13 to clerk in a hardware store. This remarkable man eventually built his own hardware store, his own manufacturing plant to make his hardware and finally a method to transport his hardware to the western frontier. He formed a railroad and expanded it until it became The New York Central Railroad. Corning 2nd was immensely proud of the man whose name he bore.

His father was Edwin Corning, an apparently quiet and bookish man who served a term as lieutenant governor of New York, an office the mayor once ran for but lost. Erastus told me he hadn't seen much of his father while growing up. It was rakish Uncle Parker who seemed to have been the young man's real mentor, which may explain his later disdain for garden clubs and high society and his attraction to a woman distinctly less sophisticated than his wife. Uncle Parker, Corning told me, also managed to lose the family fortune in the Great Depression.

My relationship with the mayor probably allowed me to go further in questioning him than other reporters might have gone, but I still thought I'd gone too far one day in an exchange that attracted the attention of Pulitzer Prize-winning author William Kennedy. That exchange was included in

Kennedy's history of his hometown, "O Albany." My question was the result of annoyance after Corning had brushed aside an issue of personal importance with an untrue answer. The Albany Common Council had a rule banning TV cameras from its meetings and was finally considering changing that rule. When I asked Corning about his position on the proposal, he answered that he would never tell the councilmen what to do. It was entirely their decision, he claimed.

"With all due respect, sir," I answered, "you hold such power in this city that if you told the councilmen to meet in pink lingerie, they would, and, at the next meeting."

Corning didn't smile, and his initial reaction worried me. "Ed, you go too far," he said. Then he added, "I think maybe blue lingerie, but pink is too much."

It was a revealing response because he didn't challenge my question's crucial assertion -- that his power in the city extended to control over the aldermen and their decisions. In his obituary, I used the clip to show how comfortable he had become in acknowledging his control over the city.

And why shouldn't he have? He'd emerged unscathed from two major investigations into his city government by the New York State Commission on Investigations, known as the SIC. One was into the practices of the police department, and the other -- more substantial and threatening -- was into the purchasing practices of his city. The latter even looked into the purchase of Corning's city-owned Oldsmobile. The bid specifications, like many others probed by the SIC, were so specific as to rule out every make and model car except the one he wanted. The commission established, I thought, at least a superficial case that most -- if not all -- so-called competitive bid specifications issued by the city were so carefully crafted that only one supplier, the one favored by the political machine, could make a successful bid. That practice, called "restrictive specifications," violates state law.

The commission, which heard all testimony under oath, finally called Erastus Corning to face interrogation by its staff of lawyers and former judges. They began with the usual groundwork status checking -- establishing that Corning was the mayor of the city and also the Albany County Democratic chairman. Then came the pointed questions about contracts, contacts and conflicts with suppliers. The mayor was in rare form. For about an hour, he evaded and dodged questions, challenged assumptions and argued over minor aspects of important issues before suddenly stopping the hearing.

"Have you been asking me these questions in my role as mayor of the city or chairman of the county Democratic committee?" Corning asked the presiding officer.

"As mayor of Albany," the retired judge answered.

"Well," said Corning. He then launched into an argument that since the last preliminary inquiry was into his status within the party he'd answered every question from that perspective and might have to change some responses to conform to his perspective as mayor. He then requested that the court stenographer read back every question and answer so he could revise whatever might be necessary. It seemed to take forever to read back all of his testimony. Late in the afternoon, after the read-back was finally completed, the chairman asked Corning if he would like to change anything.

"No," replied Corning, certainly aware that he had exhausted the major part of the time allotted for his testimony.

The entire flow of the commission's inquiry had been disrupted. The exasperated SIC chairman then adjourned the session. Corning was not recalled. The SIC left town without laying a glove on Corning's administration.

He did take criticism from the New York state comptroller for mixing funds designated for capital construction with money in the operating budget. That was the subject of my last city hall interview with him. Not much news came out of that conversation, but Corning looked healthy, so it was really surprising when he entered the hospital two days later. He'd once been a very heavy cigarette smoker and was experiencing breathing difficulties. He was expected to be discharged in a matter of days, his secretary announced.

Then, days passed and Corning remained hospitalized. Rumors began to circulate as the days turned into weeks. I had no contact with him until one Sunday evening when my wife answered the phone and, in obvious total astonishment, handed it to me and said, "It's Mayor Corning." He was calling from his hospital bed in the Albany Medical Center.

"Hello, Mayor," I said into the phone.

Corning said, "Ed, I've been lying here for weeks thinking and you were right. I've been running the city all wrong for 40 years."

I was puzzled because I'd never told him anything like that, but I detected a slur in his speech and realized that he was under the influence of some powerful drugs and was probably not thinking clearly. That impairment meant, I concluded, that this phone call was going to stay off the record. To do otherwise would violate my sense of fairness by taking advantage of someone who obviously wasn't entirely in his right mind because of medication.

His problem, Corning explained, was that no one in the city government could make a decision on his or her own. Everything came to him in the hospital to decide, and he was tired of it. So, he was thinking back to my obituary interviews and my questions about his department heads' lack of autonomy. He also wanted something of me -- to arrange a television interview to be shared with every station in town. He wanted to assure the public that he was fine.

WRGB was obviously happy to agree to a pool interview because their guy would be the one broadcast reporter in the room. Tom Bryson, the news-director at WTEN-Channel 10 News, was willing to accept the pool interview, but Jim Valentine, Bryson's counterpart at WNYT-Channel 13, was not. When Corning called me back days later, I explained that to him. I also pointed out, however, that Channel 13 had a small news audience and that channels 6 and 10 essentially covered the market. Corning agreed to the interview with just the two stations. When WNYT management understood that the interview would take place with or without their approval, they quickly joined the party.

The interview was conducted in Corning's hospital room at Albany Med. I was there with a photographer. The Albany Times Union was invited by Corning to dispatch a reporter and, I think, a still photographer. There was nothing particularly surprising said by Corning, but the images that flashed across screens all over the region quickly defeated his purpose. He looked far sicker than I'd expected, and my reaction seemed to have been shared almost universally.

My only pointed question involved the timing of his illness. He'd entered the hospital just weeks after being reelected. I asked if he'd hidden a debilitating illness from the public during his reelection campaign. He had not, he argued. He said his physical problem came on him quickly and unexpectedly. His voice was weak, his face was pale and there was no hiding the fact that he was a very sick man.

Within a few weeks, he was transferred to University hospital in Boston, where world-class pulmonary specialists could handle his care. News cameras caught his goodbye wave as he departed Albany. Some pictures taken outside the Boston hospital by various news organizations, but he gave no interviews there. He was in the Boston hospital some weeks before he contacted me again. This time, he wanted to talk about coming home.

He was improving, Corning said. He felt that he needed advice on how to manage the press when he returned. I told him that his request troubled me. I wrote a letter telling him that I saw an ethical line preventing me from instructing him on how to handle reporters and that he had to hire a press secretary for such advice. I also told him that his first interview had been a mistake because people focused entirely on his appearance and not on his words. I also advised him not to notify any reporters, including me, when he was returning. In my letter, I included some news about what had been happening in Albany during the mayor's months of absence. He sent a reply which read simply:

"*Dear Ed,*

"*Ethics are only for those not bright enough to understand the difference between right and wrong.*

"*Sincerely*

Erastus"

Unsure about exactly what that meant, I called one of his best friends, Judge John Holt-Harris, and asked if it was a put down of some sort. Not at all, Holt-Harris told me. It was one of Corning's favorite observations. Corning believed, Holt-Harris said, that formal, written ethical guidelines were needed only by people who couldn't see the shades of gray in real life situations. If you're too dumb to analyze situations shrouded in gray, he apparently believed, then and only then do you need written rules to guide you.

I heard from Corning only one more time before he died. His assistant called me at home one afternoon, said that Corning wanted to talk to me and gave me the mayor's phone number in his hospital room in Boston. I started to dial it from home, but I had an odd feeling that this might be our last conversation. So I went to the studio and fired up a tape recorder in a back production room. Then I called Boston.

Everyone who watched Corning's obituary on TV heard part of that conversation. I ended his obit with him saying goodbye. He was saying it to me, but it worked as a final message to everyone. It completed the five-minute report I'd prepared for airing upon his death, but it still wasn't enough for the station. They wanted more, felt Corning deserved more and were sure I had enough file film and tape to do more.

I prepared two more long pieces. One I called, "The Machine." The other I entitled, "The Man." I sifted through hours of file stuff. I then did some unusual production to bring it more to life. In one clip, I sat with my back to the camera in front of a plain green wall (called a chrome-key flat) and seemed to be sitting again at the back of one of Corning's news conferences from decades earlier while I showed people the mayor's techniques for dodging tough questions:

"He would interrupt me with humor," I reported on the air, "and then play to the whole room looking for another question. When that failed, he turned back to me, but not to answer my question. Rather, he dismissed it as irrelevant and moved on."

When Erastus Corning 2nd died -- on the Saturday before Memorial Day, May 28, 1983 -- I went to City Hall in Albany and introduced my three prepared pieces in a live satellite report from the sidewalk across the street. During, the broadcast, dozens of people showed up to talk to me about the mayor. Most of them were sad at his passing. A few despised him and let that be known even on the day of his death.

On the day of his funeral, I invited author William Kennedy to join me on the broadcast. Kennedy had been a newspaper reporter before turning to writing books. We both noted the most surprising scene at the church -- the presence of two grieving women to greet the mourners as they arrived for the funeral service. Just inside the church doors was Corning's widow, Elizabeth. Just outside was the woman that Kennedy and I decided to describe as Corning's confidante: Polly Noonan.

My coverage angered Corning's son, Erastus III. He let me know through intermediaries that he objected to my inclusion of personal family matters in my reporting. Specifically, he was angry that I reported his father's belief that he had failed as a father. The younger Corning also was displeased at my noting the attendance of Polly Noonan outside the church. I've never heard from him or any other Corning relative again. For my coverage, the Associated Press Broadcasters Association awarded me its top reporter prize for the year 1982.

Chapter Four: The Good

I have seen the light, and it was blue.

Of all the humans who've ever lived, only a small number have seen that light. The chance to see the Cherenkov glow was one of many rare opportunities made available to me as a result of my career in journalism. There may be no other occupation that presents as many chances to witness rare sights and encounter interesting people as does reporting. That was undoubtedly the best part of my decades of working as a general assignment reporter.

The light was at the bottom of the nuclear reactor in an electrical generating plant called Nine Mile Point. It was located near Oswego in upstate New York. The reactor vessel was open when I visited the plant, and the Cherenkov radiation was stunning to see. A vibrant and shimmering deep blue glow, it was caused by atomic particles moving through water at a speed greater than that at which light can move through water. The speed of light in a vacuum is a universal maximum, but light moves more slowly when traveling through water. Atomic particles can be pushed to speeds faster than light with a result analogous to the sonic boom caused by matter moving through air faster than sound.

What most surprised me about the open reactor was its size. It was small -- far smaller than most backyard swimming pools. Yet, the power that can be extracted from that small pool can light a city. The extraordinary power can be physically sensed when the reactor is closed and producing power. That was the case when I visited another nuclear power plant at Indian Point on the lower Hudson River. The immense power flowing through the giant turbines could be felt through my legs in the form of a vibration that seemed potent enough to shake the planet. The experience was breathtaking.

So was my landing on the *USS Saratoga*, a Forrestal class U. S. Navy aircraft carrier that displaced 80, 000 tons of water when fully loaded. I was one of about 20 journalists crammed into a Navy C-2A airplane as it slammed down on the flight deck and caught a restraining wire that pulled the aircraft to a stop. The *Saratoga* was heading home from the first Persian Gulf war when I was flown a couple of hundred miles out over the Atlantic to join it so I could cover a sailor's final night at sea. The next morning, the huge ship steamed into the Port of Jacksonville, Florida, where thousands of friends and relatives waited to greet loved ones who had been at sea for nearly eight months.

When dealing with the military in that type of situation, a journalist is considered to be an officer with the rank of major or lieutenant commander. That meant I slept in officers' quarters and ate in their mess. The enlisted sailors told me I wasn't getting the best food. The chiefs' mess was famous for having the best cuisine on the boat. It was called a boat, by the way. Most U. S. Navy ships are not, but my escorts explained that when an aviator (Navy fliers are not called pilots) looks down at a carrier, the aviator sees a boat.

My principle escort was Lt. Commander Al Vasquez from New York City. Like most military people I encountered in my career, he was politically quite conservative. He didn't like reporters, and it took a while for him to warm up to me and photographer Lou Swierzowski. What helped our relationship was the fact that he got to see areas of the Saratoga that were normally closed to junior officers. The two-star admiral held a press conference in his quarters, and Commander Vasquez had never been to that section of the ship … errr … boat. We were both surprised to see the admiral's bunk, which was a full sized four-poster bed.

My focus was on sailors from the Capital Region of New York. Late in the evening, after I interviewed local enlisted sailors in their quarters, Vasquez and his friends got into a discussion with me about press coverage of the conflict in the Gulf. He felt that all reporting in a time of war should be slanted to benefit the warriors. I finally steered him to consider press reports about the call-up of male and female reservists and the concern that the call up had effectively made some children orphans. I wanted him to complain about that affecting soldiers' morale, and he did. It should not have been covered at all, Commander Vasquez argued, because reporting on that topic hurt military morale. I went to that issue because it had been the subject of U. S. Senate hearings.

When he protested about the reporting, I was able to explain that he was actually asking the press to ignore an issue raised by the chairman of the Armed Services Committee. The commander still insisted it should not have been reported. But when I pressed him to consider the basic structure of the republic and the source of the news he wanted the press to ignore, one of his friends

interrupted and said, "Al, think about what he's saying. You've gone too far."
He actually agreed and seemed to understand some of what I'd been saying
about the complexity that a free society faces when fighting a war.

The complications I encountered in trying to tell the story of my Saratoga
visit were really unexpected. The carrier docked just after 10 in the morning. I
had a satellite window set for noon to report live on WNYT. But, the uplink
truck we'd arranged to use could not accommodate our type of video tape, so
we scrambled to find another. We did, and my report made it on air, but more
trouble followed. We'd arranged to use the editing facilities at an NBC affiliate
in Jacksonville, but the people at the station were not very helpful. They initially
stuck us in an editing suite with broken equipment. It took hours to edit our
piece for the 6 O'clock news. Then, the instructions they gave us for finding
the navy base from which we were to report at 6 O'clock were terrible.

Swierzowski and I searched for the base for over an hour and arrived just
minutes before airtime. We were met at the gate by navy shore patrol personnel.
They told us to follow them to the hanger where the satellite trucks were parked.
It was 5:55, and they drove so slowly that I was in a near panic that we would
miss our scheduled satellite window. We arrived about 30 seconds before our
scheduled time, and I heard other reporters laughing at us for having cut it so
close. We made it, though, and no one watching in Albany had an inkling that
we hadn't been at the site a just minute before we went on the air.

My White House live report was similarly desperately close to being missed.
I was there because President George H. W. Bush had hosted a Rose Garden
ceremony recognizing the newest group of "All-American Cities," which
included the City of Albany. He'd been late, and the event went much longer
than expected. So, my live report from the White House lawn at noon was an
even closer call than the Jacksonville naval base live shot had been.

Still, I got to see the White House press room and the Rose Garden. The first
thing I noticed was a wrought-iron bench sitting right where I'd expected it to
be. I had read a story about that bench and a famously aggressive ABC network
correspondent named Sam Donaldson. The claim was that Donaldson had
been relaxing on that bench one day when President Jimmy Carter suddenly
appeared in the Rose Garden just outside the door to the Oval Office. As I'd
read, the bench really was situated at the far end of the beautiful garden behind

the White House and adjoining the West Wing. The story was that Carter had been obviously agitated when he emerged from his office, gesturing and waving to all the assembled reporters except Donaldson, who was too far away on the bench.

Donaldson, it was claimed, had been instantly alarmed at what he was missing and sprang from the bench into a dead run toward Carter, but was too late. Just before the ABC correspondent could get within earshot, the President went back inside the West Wing and closed the door. Donaldson, out of breath and panting, asked the other reporters "What did he say?"

They'd all laughed and related the President's exact words. Carter had said, "Watch how fast I can get Donaldson off that bench."

Well, the bench really was there. The Rose Garden was exceptional. So was the lawn beyond it, where the Presidential helicopter awaited the President, who was to begin a Camp David vacation right after the ceremony. I was there because I was a working journalist, and I was happy to have seen it. Of course, I did not get to talk to the President.

I did get to interview Bill Clinton once. I also spent a few minutes with U. S. Senator Edward Kennedy for an interview. I interviewed Jimmy Carter before he was elected President, but my favorite time spent with a national political figure was when I was snowed in on a mountain with the dean of the U. S. Senate, George Aiken. My favorite photographer, Ken Comstock, and I had driven to Vermont to interview the senator. The snow was falling so heavily that we couldn't get to his mountaintop house. We called to explain, and Aiken told us to stay put and he would come get us.

So, I spent an entire afternoon with Aiken and his wife in his home waiting for the storm to let up. He was fascinating. He went on at some length about his famous disagreement with President Lyndon Johnson. Aiken had been an opponent of the American involvement in Vietnam and had been banned from the White House for his public pronouncements against the war. Aiken's wife made us grilled cheese sandwiches while he amazed me with his stories.

Harry Truman, I recall Aiken saying, had cried on his shoulder the day FDR died. I spent hours just listening to the senator as he talked about the history he'd experienced. It was among the most fascinating afternoons of my life. I recall telling him, when he identified people by just their first names or nicknames, that he'd have to be a bit more formal for me so I could understand who he was talking about. The George Aiken interview turned out to be one of my favorites.

My favorite interviewee was Carl Sagan. I met him when he visited RPI. We spent a couple of hours talking. He was pleased to encounter a television journalist with some science knowledge and talked about the need for more reporters with a background like mine. I understood his point because my experience was that so many journalists I knew seemed to fear science stories as inherently unfathomable. Sagan was concerned that the mainstream media consistently depicted science news as hard to understand and that displays of that attitude discouraged young people from studying science. Carl Sagan, I think, was probably the smartest person I ever interviewed. I would likely never have met him and surely would not have spent so much time with him had I not been a reporter.

Chapter Five: TV Consultants

"Live, Local, Late-Breaking." That slogan became nationally famous because the biggest research firm in the television news business saw it work at WNYT.

A representative from Magid Inc., Ron Turner, was in the room at television station WNYT in Albany on the morning I first proposed the newscast changes that gave rise to the slogan. It was mostly my response to what the market research his firm had presented to the station's management the day before. I was there in my role as managing editor of the newscasts. On-air performers are generally not invited to discussions with consultants. The on-air people are rarely allowed to see the results of research on themselves and never are permitted access to research done on other performers. That results in a narrowing of the discussion afterward because performers understand the business from a unique perspective that should be considered.

The use of market research about news broadcasters was pioneered by the late Frank Magid's Cedar Rapids, Iowa firm in the 1950s. Their colored charts and graphs were always interesting to view even if the general message was often unpleasant to absorb. My first experience with a Magid market research project, nearly 30 years earlier, had nearly cost me my career. The message of that report was explicit: It was, "Replace Ed Dague at 6 and 11." Magid delivered it to the Schenectady station (WRGB), where my television anchoring career had begun barely three months before. The station management concluded that Magid's finding was premature.

At that time, in 1976, the Magid consultant handling the WRGB account was a 30-something man named Richard Sabreen. He had me travel to Cedar Rapids in 1977 to spend two days being coached by the Magid staff on the finer points of anchoring news. The firm had a standard set of drills, and students were taped while doing them. The students and coaches then critiqued the performances on the tapes and, if necessary, repeated the process. One exercise involved sitting at an anchor desk and delivering a news broadcast while keeping one's arms raised high. The point was to demonstrate the ill effects of locking one's elbows on the anchor desk while performing. Some of the exercises were useful. The ones demonstrating the relationship between reading speed and facial expressions were amazing to me.

A colleague of mine at WRGB, William Fortune Snyder (on-air name, Bill Fortune), had gone to Magid's "Anchor School" a year or so before I attended. The oddity involved was that Snyder had been told before leaving for school that he had lost his job as WRGB's late newscast anchor. While he went to Magid's school anyway, he returned full of anger about losing his position and decided in favor of an on-air protest. That worried me because I was producing the newscast and feared I might be fired for failing to rein in Fortune's final fusillade.

He told me just before going on air that he understood the Magid method completely and would carry the hand and facial gestures to an extreme while yelling out the scripted words as quickly as he could. It was hard to watch.

The control room exploded in laughter the moment he started. I sat there with the technicians, wondering what kind of reaction this outrageous performance would draw. The last thing I expected was that it would draw praise. But that's exactly what happened. News director Don Decker called after the newscast and commented on how animated Bill Snyder had seemed. Decker was pleased, I was amazed and Snyder was still out of the anchor chair.

We all presumed that it was the result of the consultant's market research, but only management saw that secret report. My routine exposure to the full market research presentations didn't begin until I moved to WNYT in 1984. It was sometimes unpleasant to hear critics' verbatim comments about my performance, but I had learned to handle the nastiest of comments back in 1969, after my first few months on air. The research was disappointing because of what it said about viewers. People didn't want much serious news; government and international stories were boring. Eventually, we understood that to improve our ratings we had to dumb-down our newscasts.

When I joined Channel 13, the station was already using a Magid competitor out of Dallas, Texas, a firm called Audience Research and Development, generally referred to as AR&D. Their top guy was a former Magid manager named Ed Bewly. His presentations of the annual market research were inevitably discouraging. WNYT was doing "The Thirty Minute

News" in the mid 1980s, drawing contrast to the two major competitors' hour long newscasts. It wasn't working for the station. Ratings were increasing but too slowly. Bewly told us that we were running a boutique for educated viewers when we needed to open a K-Mart for the mass of viewers.

Actually, he presented it statistically. The chance that a viewer with college graduate credits would tune to WNYT for news was over 80 per cent. Chances of a viewer without a high school degree watching WNYT were around 20 per cent. No one ever explicitly advised us to dumb it down, but we got the message and that's what we did. It's actually cheaper and easier to cover less complicated stories. Political and legislative reporting require some expertise, but almost anyone can cover a fire or car crash.

It worked. It didn't take WNYT to the very top of the market, but the number of viewers did increase when we focused more on so-called "hard news" than on politics and legislation. I used to tell the staff that if we aired the best newscast in the history of mankind and no one watched it, then we would have achieved exactly nothing. An audience was essential, and consultants like Sabreen and Bewly put absolute faith in their research. A decade after Richard Sabreen had recommended my replacement as anchor at WRGB when he was working for Magid, he offered me a job with Group W Broadcasting, where he had become vice president for News. I asked him if he recalled telling WRGB to dump me and whether that didn't seem inconsistent with the offer he'd just extended.

"Oh, no," I recall him saying. "I always thought you were doing a great job. It was the research numbers that didn't agree."

Many consultants viewed their research that way, as absolute reflections of market realities.

At WNYT, market research first caused me a problem then provided a solution. It all started with the departure of co-anchor Nancy Cozean, who later ended up as mayor of Poughkeepsie, N.Y. She had been at WNYT when I arrived, but seemed to tire of anchoring after the first few years. WNYT did offer her a contract renewal, but the station wanted her to move to Albany. Cozean drove a hundred miles each day to work at WNYT. Her husband worked in New York City, so the couple had bought a house situated between their two jobs, in Poughkeepsie. Cozean had made the long drive up the Taconic Parkway for years. When WNYT insisted that she move to Albany she left to work at an upstart station in Kingston, south of Albany and closer to Poughkeepsie. That was when my problem began.

WNYT decided not to hire a new co-anchor -- that I could anchor both major newscasts alone. The idea appeared to come up spontaneously at a management meeting, but I realized later it had been a set-up. I did not want to anchor alone. I thought the consultant would quickly squash the notion, so I insisted that Bewly be called. I realized quickly that he had been in on the single anchor idea all along.

"There are no negatives, Ed," he kept repeating. "There are no negatives."

He meant that the research on me showed no real audience dislike of me. My positives weren't world-beating, but there was no negative feeling at all toward me, according to his statistics. The single anchor idea was supported by the research, in his opinion. So, I became the sole anchor of WNYT's 6 and 11 O'clock newscasts. It was hard work. There was a lot of reading. Transitions between types of stories were less smooth. Too many stories in a row by a single anchor could sound like endless droning and needed more than just a camera change for variety.

The next year, there were some negatives in my personal scores and even more in the research project the year after that. That ended it, and I won my argument for a co-anchor. The research couldn't say who should be named to anchor with me, but it did clearly identify the problem inherent in a single anchor newscast. The show became sterile. With no on-set human interaction, broadcasters' personalities became flat and less humanity showed through to the viewers. When I saw the rising negatives in my personal research numbers I understood the dynamic, and I found that the research could be used persuasively to bolster my argument.

The research that prompted "Live, Local, Late Breaking" was also persuasive. It had kept me awake in thought for much of the night preceding my proposal. Before the management conference, I explained my ideas to news-director Steve Baboulis. He, in turn, introduced me to the management group when he was asked to present ideas about the research results. I told them "I want to do a late newscast called "Live at Eleven" based on a concept of "Live, Local, Late Breaking." The idea, I explained, was to lay claim to the very traits where the viewing audience saw us as having deficiencies.

Which station would you tune to for the latest news during an emergency? Which station had the most local news? Which station seemed to update its news between newscasts? Audience answers to questions like that were generally not favorable to WNYT, but the viewer response provided a clear opportunity for recruiting new viewers. The promises made -- to present newscasts filled with live, local and late-breaking stories -- are fairly easy to appear to keep.

We moved a few staffers, including our top producers, from days to nights and held our lead story slot open as late as possible. We rolled the live trucks toward any breaking news. Our lead was always live, and that made it always local. The challenge was in making sure that the lead story would be so recent as to be still a bit unknown, which could obscure the fact that our lead story was sometimes trivial. We put an intern on-air from a newsroom desk covered with police scanners for a summary of ongoing police calls. We emphasized what consultant research told us viewers believed wc did poorly, and viewers responded by watching in overwhelming numbers.

Chapter Six: Unions and the News

Unions had once been much more powerful at radio and television stations than they were when I first encountered them at WGY in 1969. The economic realities in a swiftly changing and highly technological business made it difficult for the broadcast unions to prosper. Their jurisdictional restrictions often were quickly made irrelevant by rapidly advancing technology. Today, processes that were once limited to technicians by labor contract can now be performed by anyone with access to a newsroom computer.

When I joined the staff of General Electric Broadcasting, two broadcast unions still had substantial power. They were NABET, the National Association of Broadcast Employees and Technicians, which represented the news cameramen and station technical employees, and AFTRA, the American Federation of Television and Radio Artists. AFTRA handled labor issues for reporters and announcers. The station management viewed the unions much like GE's managers at the turbine factory downtown might view their unions. My frustration toward the attitudes of the G. E. Broadcasting managers grew steadily during my 15 years with the company. The station hired responsible and intelligent people to go out into the community and cover every aspect of life then treated those same people like children who were incapable of understanding the business they were in or the policies of the firm that employed them.

"Me boss, you peon." That was how a colleague categorized the managerial culture at the stations. My biggest complaint was the sheer cheapness of the operation and the lies told about it in the promotional announcements on air every day. The amount of profit being squeezed out of the Schenectady broadcast operation was exorbitant, in my view. A bundle of money was being made because of a government-granted monopoly on a limited public resource -- the radio spectrum.

That was generally the case across the whole business, it was alleged by people like Newton Minow, who chaired the Federal Communications Commission for President John F. Kennedy. In 1961, a month before I graduated high school, Minnow famously labeled broadcast television a "vast wasteland." My hopes for having a meaningful impact on our society through my career were lost every day in the compromises that were made necessary by desperate battles against unyielding deadlines. There was too little corporate commitment to journalism and to serving the community. Staffing levels were shamefully low. I felt almost guilty of fraud at times for presenting programs that were advertised as being far more than what was theoretically possible with the meager resources allocated.

There was nothing I could do about the prevailing business model for local TV stations. I battled with management for staff overtime, and I often disagreed with coverage decisions. So, it made perfect sense that I should be elected head of the local AFTRA chapter to sanction my battles with management. I was elected union president in the early 1970s.

Shortly thereafter, WGY decided to fire mid-day host Harry Downie. Then, they decided not to. Actually, Downie threatened the management with a loss of his sponsors, and management caved in. The supermarket chain Grand Union was the big account Downie told the managers he could persuade to withdraw from WGY. The decision to fire Downie was rescinded. The trouble was that they'd already hired his replacement.

Hy Agens was his name, and when I first entered the dispute Agens was driving to Schenectady with his whole family to start his new job.

So, WGY management decided to fire another guy. Steve Sullivan was doing the important afternoon show -- known as "afternoon drive" in the business. His ratings were good, he had given management no grief. There was absolutely no prior indication that his job was at all shaky. Still, he was summarily fired under the union contract's so called "suitability clause" and given two weeks pay for every year he had worked at the station.

I couldn't help him. I did file a grievance and won a concession that, in the future, no one could be fired under the labor contract's suitability clause without some prior indication by management of dissatisfaction with the performer's work. In 1986, long after I had moved to WNYT, I was called to testify at an arbitration hearing about the "Sullivan Amendment," which was still operative in the WGY labor contract with AFTRA.

There was one job I did save. Manager-News Don Decker decided to fire reporter Jim Williams around 1974. I had fought with Decker about Williams many times. The first time in 1970 was about my decision to have Williams handle more feature stories than hard news events. He was good at reporting those; his natural warmth and humanity showed clearly on such stories. When fired, he had been working the evening radio news shift, for which he was eminently unsuitable. He was in Don Decker's penalty box.

Then WRGB decided to expand its evening newscast to one hour, the first such newscast in the market. The station planned to hire three new staffers, and the need to replace Williams made the number of total prospective hires four. I was able to convince Decker that no one in the management side of broadcast news was so perceptive that they could hire four people and be sure that each one was better than Jim Williams. The new newscast would need strong feature reporters, I argued. Jim Williams was unfired. But, he knew where he stood and left less than a year later to try other jobs in television. He had some success doing national commercials for a while. He was a good guy and a decent reporter who struggled with hard news because there was often little available for story telling besides cold and sometimes tragic factual information. Williams sometimes had trouble with facts.

Saving Jim Williams from being fired was nice, but the big part of my union work was negotiating a new contract. With that assignment, I had help in the form of Walter Grinspan. He was the AFTRA business agent who'd bedeviled GE Broadcasting management for at least a decade previous. I had first met him shortly after I started with the station in 1969. There was a strike by the technicians, and AFTRA voted to honor the NABET picket line. I think the strike lasted nine days, but it was not a big deal to me. As I recall the incident, Martha Brooks, a retired radio icon, prevailed at the one union meeting I attended after she joined Grinspan in opposing taking a vote on crossing the NABET picket lines. Grinspan was smart, bold and blunt, and I loved working with him. My contract negotiations probably marked the beginning of the end for me at WRGB.

Grinspan wanted a show of support at the round of contract talks held a year before I was elected union leader. I went as well to see General Electric's new labor relations head, their supposed big gun, James J. Delmonico, who'd just been brought in from Syracuse. He'd been opposing unions there for General Electric for a decade or more at the light bulb division. He knew nothing about broadcasting. When Grinspan started arguing for a raise for WGY's morning star, Bill Edwardsen, he talked about Edwardsen's high ratings affecting station advertising rates. That was when Delmonico, employee relations Manager for General Electric Broadcasting Co., interrupted and said, "Now wait a minute! Do you mean that we charge more for commercials at one time of day than we do at other times?"

Within three years, just in time for the next contract renegotiation cycle, Jim Delmonico had been made VP of GE Broadcasting and general manager of WGY/WRGB/WGFM, the whole shebang on Balltown Road in Schenectady. As one result, Delmonico did not handle the contract talks. Instead, he brought in his young assistant, Greg Oswald, who had been promoted to manager of employee relations. We got along fine and rewrote virtually the entire agreement to strip out provisions from a bygone era of broadcasting. The only difficulties arose during the negotiations about pay rates. Something happened during that discussion that, I was told later by Operations Manager Charlie King, convinced the company that I really would lead the announcers out on strike. It was a misperception arising from pain.

During a discussion about salaries, I'd gotten up from the bargaining table and gone to the window that looked out on a rainy city street. I was still listening but had said all I wanted to say and simply could sit no longer. My back was on fire. It hurt so much that my eyes watered, so I faced the window. My disease had not been correctly diagnosed at that point, so no one, including me, knew what was going on. Only I understood that the intense pain wouldn't allow me to sit. So, I just stood there for a very long time. The company representatives took my several hours at the window as evidence of my intransigence on the money issues and met in Delmonico's office that evening to revise their money offer.

When the new contract was signed, Delmonico told the whole non-union staff at the station that they wouldn't get raises on time because AFTRA had taken too much. That meant that every director, secretary, janitor, etc. viewed me as the guy who'd taken their pay raises away.

There was never any hope of negotiating a new benefit like vacation time. Our labor agreement tied AFTRA's benefits directly to those received by the IUE --- General Electric's main union --- the International Union of Electrical workers. That link was explicit in the contract language. So, when Delmonico called me and the NABET union leader, Fred Saburro, to his office after GE had signed a new agreement with the IUE, I expected to learn what the big union had gotten. Instead, we were told that we would not be getting the IUE's package. When I objected, Delmonico grew furious and threw me out of his office.

He apologized hours later and explained that he wanted some concession from NABET and got overly upset when AFTRA gave him trouble. That reinforced my problem with him. He was always playing games, always trying to scam someone somehow, and it was difficult to trust him. Near the end of a long and difficult telethon for muscular dystrophy one year, he told me it didn't matter whether we raised more than we had the past year because he would put up a bigger number even if it was untrue. He would just lie to viewers.

On another occasion, when I complained about the station including live feature reports from DisneyWorld without revealing that the Disney Company was paying for the station's expenses for the series of reports, he was puzzled by my point. His response was, "How would anybody ever know?". The Disney reports amounted to commercials, and the practice of allowing sponsors to buy news coverage troubled him not at all, it seemed.

Jim Delmonico was the man I quit at WRGB, and the single driving reason was my belief that I couldn't trust him. When he sold out to investment leverage buyout specialist Forstmann Little and Company by forcing a strike by his station's technicians in 1984, so he could break their union and savage their labor contract, I found work with what I thought was a more responsible operation. The labor negotiators for the company and the union (NABET) had reached an agreement on a new contract in 1984, but Delmonico rejected it. It appeared that he'd deliberately forced the technicians' union to strike. There was no indication from Delmonico that he wanted a peaceful labor settlement. As it turned out, the month-long strike by the technicians and cameramen ended with the striking union, NABET, severely weakened and the decades long alliance between the station's two unions shattered.

That action by AFTRA, the union I'd led as president in previous contract disputes, disturbed me a great deal. It was not just the end of the alliance between unions but also the end of democracy within the performers' union.

As with my first strike experience more than a decade earlier, a meeting was called after a week of honoring NABET picket lines to vote on whether AFTRA members would cross the lines the following week. There was no vote because several union members said they were going to cross the lines no matter how AFTRA voted. Jack Aernecke and Ernie Tetrault were afraid they would lose their jobs if they didn't cross. It marked another appearance of the insecurity that's so pervasive in broadcasting. Tetrault and Aernecke were not let go, but people who spoke in favor of continuing to honor the technician's pickets, like Brian Burnell and his wife Susan Barnett, were gone within a year. Of course, so was I.

Chapter Seven: Conventions

It took me a long time to read U. S. Senator Alfonse D'Amato's lips. I was in San Diego for the 1996 Republican National Convention, and Senator D'Amato was the acknowledged boss of New York Republican politics. He'd gotten my attention by forcefully shoving a dais microphone away before talking to the party's soon-to-be presidential nominee, Kansas Senator Robert Dole. Whatever D'Amato said to Dole, he made it too obvious that he wanted no one to hear it. That, in turn, made me all the more curious about what had been said so surreptitiously by D'Amato. I couldn't hear it, but I could see it.

I had tape of the brief exchange, and I could see D'Amato's face clearly. My cameraman had continuing taping well past the end of the morning breakfast caucus at which Dole had addressed the New York delegation. On the way back to our temporary facilities near the convention hall, I'd complained to the crew about having to carry the damned tripod everywhere we went. Hours later I apologized, after realizing that I was watching D'Amato's lips move on rock steady video because our camera had been mounted on that very tripod.

So, I watched the video over and over, sometimes in slow motion, until I was sure what D'Amato had said to Dole: "Pataki was great on Sunday," was one D'Amato comment that was very clear once I managed to read the senator's lips on the tape. The rest of what D'Amato told Dole was harder to read.

I could make out D'Amato saying, "You've got to let …"Kemp."

I couldn't get the next few words, but D'Amato definitely ended by saying the name "Kemp." Then, I understood. D'Amato was trying to convince Dole to let New York Governor George Pataki, D'Amato's prime protégé, make the nominating speech for Dole's vice-presidential choice – former Buffalo-area Congressman Jack Kemp. Pataki had addressed the New York delegation at their hotel on Sunday evening and had given a far more rousing speech than anybody was used to seeing from him.

So I put together a story showing what D'Amato had tried to arrange. I inserted my own voice reconstructing D'Amato's words just as he mouthed them. It turned out even better when D'Amato pulled off his coup on behalf of Pataki. Hours later, when the Dole campaign announced that Kemp's name would be placed in nomination by Pataki, I had a report ready to show how

Pataki had gotten the assignment. When news of the Pataki selection moved on the wires, I got across the street and onto the convention floor before the news reached the New York delegation. My photographer rolled his camera tape as I told the state chairman about Pataki's upcoming moment in the national spotlight, then gestured toward his delegation and said, "Tell them." The chairman did. The delegates reacted on camera.

I had two interesting pieces of tape ready for the upcoming live broadcast back in Albany. There was time for a third tape in my newscast cut-in, since the D'Amato lobbying piece and the wild sound of New York delegates hearing then cheering the news of Pataki's selection were brief items. The third item would allow me to contrast the treatment of GOP insider Pataki with that given GOP outsider, Governor William Weld of Massachusetts. He'd been rudely welcomed and encouraged to leave earlier in the day. I had a good interview and visual story on that. Now, if I could ad-lib a live narrative connecting the three items and do it from the middle of the bustling convention floor to a camera situated so far away that I could barely see it, I would have delivered to my audience something I believed had value.

It was my turn to use the "floor cam," a small video camera mounted on the underside of a high network camera scaffold half way across the arena. NBC's Newschannel, a consortium of NBC-affiliated stations, had positioned a wireless microphone and earpiece 'IFB' [1]in an aisle somewhere near the Ohio delegation sign. WNYT had paid a substantial sum to be part of the Newschannel operation. The floor cam was one of the benefits of being with the group, assuming we could find the consortium's equipment in that crowded arena.

Just before 11, my producer, Eric Hoppel, and I pushed our way through the sea of bodies in the hot San Diego convention center to a location next to the Ohio delegation where we found the gear for the Newschannel link. I was sweating and struggling to make myself look presentable and joking about it with Ohio Lieutenant Governor Nancy Hollister, who was standing next to me. She began fanning me with her large "DOLE" sign, and other delegates

---

[1] IFB is jargon for the earpiece worn by TV performers and stands for "Internal FeedBack"

joined her as I began reporting live to Albany.

I could hear my co-anchor's introduction, and I could hear the audio on my taped pieces coming back at me from Albany right on cue. My producer had given the Albany show producer three "roll cues" for those reports. Those were key words I intended to utter in my on-camera narrative to signal the Albany control room to roll the reports that they'd received a half hour earlier on a closed satellite feed from San Diego.

A report of this sort happens live, and it happens just once. It was a performance based on a mental draft of a narrative script intended to get me into and out of prepared reports. In support, there was producer Hoppel crouched below camera view shouting out times and cues, but there was no teleprompter, no written script and no notes. There were about 100,000 people watching at home in Albany, and if they got the impression that what I was doing was in any way hard to do then I would be doing it wrong.

I found it to be fun in the way that any competitive performance can be enjoyable when it goes well. It was the best aspect of television news reporting under one roof and packed into one week. The days were always long, and each was a rollicking mixture of strange and fascinating encounters and events. In the 20 years between 1976 and 1996, I covered five national political nominating conventions. Each was made radically different from the one before by the rapidly changing technology of electronic journalism.

At my first convention, in 1976, my station (WRGB) was still using film. My reports to Albany were transmitted via Greyhound Bus Lines in sealed canisters of undeveloped film. My seat was a pile of telephone books in a back hallway in Madison Square Garden, and my dominant memory is of being advised what not to photograph.

While working on a story about what local convention delegates did after the sessions ended, I was in the New York delegation's hotel about to shoot film of several delegates having drinks in the bar just off the lobby. That was when a friend tapped me on the shoulder and said, "Ed, that is a picture we generally don't take."

The friend was Arvis Chalmers, a longtime print columnist for the now-departed Albany Knickerbocker News. Chalmers covered the New York State Legislature and Capitol. The picture he warned me not to take was of Erastus

Corning 2nd, Albany's mayor. What Chalmers noticed was that Corning was sitting with Polly Noonan, his presumed girlfriend. I didn't use the pictures.

Four years later, the Democrats again held their national convention at Madison Square Garden and again nominated Jimmy Carter for President. New York Governor Hugh Carey opposed Carter. Instead, Carey favored nominating Senator Edward Kennedy of Massachusetts. The night before a critical rules vote, I talked to Carey in the hotel lobby and quickly realized he was quite drunk. He was pleasant and willing to talk, but his eyes could not quite focus on me and he needed support from a column in the lobby.

I was impressed because, as inebriated as he was, Carey still was able to mount a coherent argument for continuing what was clearly a doomed struggle. Carey talked about historical figures who'd espoused other lost causes and stood for principle. He likened himself to Thomas Becket, a 12th Century cleric who was murdered by assassins acting for King Henry II of England. Governor Carey's conclusion was that even though Becket lost his fight, he is remembered by history for having fought for a conviction. Carey evidently thought history would remember him for fighting to unbind delegates to state primary winners even though he knew he was sure to lose.

I'd approached Carey with a reporter from WTEN-Channel 10, Bob Lawson. Lawson had been the news-director I'd called into work at 3 in the morning on the night that Robert Kennedy had been fatally shot and I'd been fired. Lawson had worked at WGY for a while before moving to television and its "Eyewitness News" format. One of the factors that made conventions such interesting events for me was the chance to visit with people in the business. Bob Lawson was one of my favorite characters in broadcast journalism. He had great local contacts and a very distinctive voice.

The 1980 Convention was also where another friend in the business advised me to get out of it because "this business will break your heart". His name was Wilson Hall, and it had once been a famous name in broadcasting. Hall had been a radio network foreign correspondent who'd covered stories from the revolution of Fidel Castro in Cuba to the war in Vietnam. His career had been brilliant, but the radio networks withered and Hall found that there were no jobs for radio correspondents after about 1975. He turned to television in desperation, but he could not save his career. In 1978, Hall took a job as the main news anchor at Channel 13 in Albany, which was then operating as WAST. By the 1980 convention, he'd been told his contract wouldn't be renewed. We had become friends and, I was saddened to see him so defeated.

Larry King of CNN was not a friend of mine. I'm sure he had no clue as to who I was when he promised to get back at me at one of the conventions. I was in need of a comment on something big from Mario Cuomo while he was still governor of New York. Cuomo was scheduled to appear on King's CNN show from the arena, so I staked out the hallway by King's studio. King came out once, looked around rather frenetically, saw me and knew I was waiting for Cuomo.

"Don't you stop him," he yelled to me. "He's late for my show, and don't you stop him for an interview."

I didn't. Cuomo turned into the hallway followed by some aides, saw me and walked straight over. He said, "What have you got, Ed?" I raised the hand-microphone and got a fairly brief comment. I didn't ask a follow-up question, but even that was too much for King. During what I presume was a commercial break, he opened the studio door again and shouted, "I told you not to stop him. I'll get you for that." He never did, of course.

One of the benefits of working in television journalism in a state capitol is that many powerful figures know and recognize you. That was what caused Cuomo to stop on his way to the King interview and what I presume drew New York Lieutenant Governor Betsy McCaughey Ross to my breakfast table during the first few days of the GOP Convention in San Diego in 1996. She joined me and my producer asking for information about how to make some trouble. I knew only a little bit, but what I knew stopped her cold.

Betsy McCaughey made been a politically active academic who'd made herself famous with a "New Republic" magazine article that was highly critical of Bill and Hillary Clinton's health care proposals. George Pataki had not met her before offering to make her his running mate. He dumped her after one term, and she again achieved some national prominence by writing the first article claiming that Barack Obama's health care reform proposal provided for federal death panels. In 1996, at my breakfast table, she wanted to know how to oppose a GOP party platform plank.

Why me? I didn't know anything beyond the general idea of filing a minority report and having it voted on by the full convention. I told her that some minimum number of state delegations had to sign on to her idea as a first step. I believe that her concern was over an abortion issue, and I did report on her interest in opposing the party platform plank.

She returned the following morning for a discussion I'll always remember because I could see her deflate when I told her that I believed that the end process in presenting a minority plank for adoption was for her to take the podium and defend her proposal before the delegates voted. It was so obvious that the thought of addressing the entire convention so terrified her that I knew with certainty that there would be no minority plank submission.

I was right. It was her last breakfast with us.

Chapter Eight: Co-Anchors

The Olympic downhill gold medal race in 1976 was won by skier Franz Klammer. Liz Bishop was handling the sports report on WRGB-Channel 6 the day after the race. She wrote a lead-in script for her segment to be read by Ernie Tetrault. It said simply:

"IN SPORTS, WHO WILL EVER FORGET THE PERFORMANCE OF FRANZ KLAMMER? HERE'S LIZ WITH THE FULL SPORTS REPORT."

But, instead, Tetrault misread the lead-in and said: "In Sports, who will ever forget the performance of Frank Clammer?"

On air, Bishop immediately responded, "Well, obviously you!" and burst out laughing. A lot of television anchors would have been mortified to have a mistake laughed at by a colleague on set. Not Tetrault, and that self-effacing quality in him greatly influenced the ease and genuine nature of interactions that viewers saw within that 1970s group of people on the Channel 6 set. Tetrault was easy to work with and never a liability. We had a lot of fun together, and it showed.

We sat facing each other in the newsroom at WRGB for most of a decade. We shared a lot of frustration about the diminishing quality of our product caused by an ever-expanding workload. Tetrault decided one day that, as far as the management was concerned, we were making doughnuts. There was no evidence of concern about quality of reporting. Instead, all the focus seemed to be on quantity

"Gotta make the doughnuts," he would proclaim as he sat across from me to type scripts.

After I quit WRGB, I felt bad for Tetrault because he should have been making much more money than he was. He never understood his value to WRGB and was very timid when dealing with management. He told me years afterward that when the managers I had quit called him to the front office because WRGB's late news ratings were slipping, he'd been convinced that they were going to fire him. He told me he was so relieved when they asked him to return to co-anchoring the late news that he never asked for a raise for doing the extra broadcast.

His co-anchor after I left was Liz Bishop, who'd begun anchoring news just a year or so before my departure. She joined me as co-anchor at 11 O'clock. She was the first female anchor at WRGB and was initially uneasy, I thought, because she'd moved from sports to news. She shouldn't have been. Liz was intelligent, had a strong on-air presence and was a good storyteller. She was a solid anchor, and her mistreatment by the boss triggered the phone call that lead me to quit WRGB.

Bishop was crying at her desk when I returned to the newsroom after the dinner break one evening in May of 1984. She'd come back just minutes before me and had stopped to talk with the pickets walking the NABET line outside the studio during a strike that was then in its second week. She'd been seen by management as she'd spoken with the picketers and threatened with the loss of her job if she ever again stopped to chat at the picket line. I called the boss, Don Decker, angry about the emotional pain he'd caused Liz. I was given the absurd argument that he'd acted to protect Bishop's appearance of impartiality. My next call was to Steve Baboulis, then the assistant news director at WNYT.

When I made the move to Channel 13 eight weeks later I was concerned about my reception. After all, my move to that station had caused the Channel 13 to terminate anchor Craig Alexander, who presumably had friends in the WNYT newsroom. He did not, it seems. He'd made enemies by taunting Wilson Hall in the newsroom after he'd taken over Hall's anchor position. Craig, whom I'd never met, had alienated other staffers by inserting his own radical religious beliefs in place of scripted news on at least one occasion. Lead producer Leslie Moran explained Alexander's estrangement from the staff to me on my very first day at the station.

After a six month period off air, on December 2, 1984, I began co-anchoring WNYT's newscasts with Nancy Cozean. She'd been at the station for years and, through her competent presentation, had held what meager ratings WNYT had managed to attract at that point. Cozean was smooth on air, but she could become distracted and prone to mistakes at times. Once, without noticing, she read the same story I'd just finished reading. Her 1985 election night performance severely damaged her image with the management as she appeared to have done no studying for the broadcast at all. She stumbled through the entire presentation.

There was a reason for her inconsistency, I thought. It was fatigue. She drove to Albany from Poughkeepsie every day and back every night. She was a working mother with a too-busy schedule, and it was hampering her performance. We never achieved the sort of closeness I had with every other co-anchor in my career, so her decision to leave for a new station in Kingston was rumored but never discussed with me.

The management decision not to replace Cozean but, instead, to have me anchor alone was something I opposed. After about 18 months of solo anchoring at 6 and 11, the management finally decided to add a co-anchor. The big issue was who it would be. There were two obvious candidates on staff, Chris Kapostasy and Benita Zahn. Both had been appearing regularly on the 6 O'clock news as specialists. Zahn was the health reporter, and Kapostasy was the consumer (we called it "money") specialist. I had a very firm opinion on which should be made co-anchor, but it was not shared universally among the management deciders.

My choice was Chris Kapostasy. Steve Baboulis, who'd risen to news director by that point, agreed with me, but the general manager, the consultant and the promotion manager wanted Zahn to at least split the duties with Kapostasy. There was precedent in the market for switching co-anchors between newscasts, but Baboulis and I felt one consistent team was better for audience acceptance. Before the final management meeting on the topic, Baboulis and I went across the street to a restaurant to plan a strategy. We both recognized that Baboulis could hurt his career in management by taking too firm a stand of this issue. I, on the other hand, could afford to insist forcefully because I wasn't going anywhere in the management hierarchy.

We got our way without my having to insist. Kapostasy got the job. When General Manager Don Perry announced the promotion, he called Kapostasy to his office, told her that we'd decided to add an anchor and she was it. He added that it was Ed's decision. He then summoned Benita Zahn to his office and told her the same thing -- including that it had been Ed's decision. Minutes after the meeting ended, Zahn was in my office in tears wanting to know why.

It was a matter of human chemistry, I told her. Kapostasy and I were more alike in style of presentation, and my comfort level would be higher with her,

I told Benita. It hurt Benita, and that saddened me because she was a strong reporter and solid performer and I feared she'd quit the station. She thought about it, I know, but didn't. As I write this book, some years later, Zahn is now the anchor of WNYT's six O'clock news.

The Kapostasy decision was the correct one, as history proved. We anchored together for 11 years and secured the number one rating at both 6 and 11 before she left in 1998 to join NBC's new venture at MSNBC as Chris Jansing. I was very sad to see her leave. We'd developed a close personal friendship and a professional relationship that was never uneasy. Our on-air presentation was so practiced that we could finish each other's sentences. We understood the other's moods even when nothing showed, as on the night I asked her almost immediately after the opening tease, "What's wrong?"

"Hans died tonight," she answered, telling me of the expected loss of her old and sick dachshund. Viewers could not see her pain, I am convinced, but I knew it after her first on-air sentence.

WNYT's management decided to replace Kapostasy with someone from outside the market. I had little to do with that search. I could have vetoed their selection of Kari Lake, but I had no reason to do that.

Lake came to Albany from the Fox affiliate in Phoenix, Arizona. Her husband was a photographer, and WNYT hired him as well. That had more to do with her abbreviated tenure at Channel 13 than any other single factor, I think. There were immediate union problems that grew steadily over Lake's year and a half at the station. Lake did not have to join the union (NABET), but her husband did. WNYT was a closed shop.

In my time as union president at WRGB, the national union had consistently ordered me to push for a closed shop, and I'd just as consistently refused. I don't believe that anyone should have to join a union to hold a job, but it was always easier for a company to agree to a closed shop than to fight it. After all, it didn't affect the station ownership in the slightest. In news broadcasting, the Supreme Court of the United States had ruled (in Buckley vs. AFTRA) that a reporter could not be forced to join a union.

At WNYT, only Kari Lake, me and meteorologist Norm Sebastian had declined union membership. Lake's husband, Jeff, was subject to the union's seniority rules in the critical issue of vacation scheduling. That made it most difficult for the pair to schedule days off together. When the management bent the union rules to allow Jeff and Kari simultaneous vacations, Jeff took serious heat from fellow photographers. It became nasty as co-workers first insulted and then shunned him. He was the one who first became really unhappy working at WNYT because of the abuse he was taking from his fellow photographers. He wanted out, she followed. He quit before she did and went back to Phoenix.

Lake believed that she had a three-year contract with WNYT with an escape clause that became operative half way into it. So, after a year and a half as my co-anchor, Kari Lake agreed to return to her old station in Phoenix. WNYT wouldn't let her go. The general manager by that time was Steve Baboulis, and I found him to be intransigent on the question of Kari Lake's contract, which he interpreted as having no escape clause. Lake, who had been confiding in me all through her tenure at the station, became increasingly distraught.

Back in Phoenix, she told me, her station had erected billboards announcing her return, and she was in a bind. It became an emotional travail for her. Pressure from Phoenix met obstinacy in Albany, and Lake started to crack. She was increasingly disliked by the staff, many of whom were gung-ho unionists, and by the management, who started to view her as a spoiled brat. Lake called in sick for days at a time. When she did come to work, there were many days when I had to console her at some length to get her crying stopped so she could perform on air. Once, I couldn't manage that, so she stayed behind at her desk in the newsroom, sobbing, while I anchored alone. I felt awful for her. She was much younger than she appeared on air – just a kid caught in a helpless bind with possible lawsuits being filed against her by two TV stations.

On one awful 6 O'clock newscast, Kari Lake was so distraught that she couldn't read the script. Every story she read contained a stumble or two. She read slowly, trying to compensate, but that made the performance worse. Sitting next to her on the set, I knew that she knew it. By contrast, I was having a very good performance, and I knew it, which made it harder for her. The comparison between us was so striking that several viewers called me during the show to leave messages complaining that I was trying to show her up. I'd expected that, but I couldn't do anything to prevent it. I slowed down my reading a bit, but I wasn't going to start deliberately stumbling over words to diminish the comparison. Her problem became public when newspaper media reporters starting writing about it. Then a local radio talk show host named Mike Gallagher started savaging her with horribly mean comments.

Finally, after having no success at mediating between management and Lake, I made a public comment supporting her. I told a print reporter that I was tempted to start picketing the station if they didn't free Kari. That did it. They let her go but got very angry with me. I found it strange because Steve Baboulis had understood my point about unhappy anchors when I'd quit WRGB. In a nutshell, I believe that when a performer decides that he or she no longer want to perform for a station it is folly to attempt to force a performance.

Now, WNYT had to replace Kari Lake. The management and consultants found three candidates. I had lunch with all three and found the decision to be fairly easy. Lydia Kulbida was undoubtedly the smartest candidate and the most experienced. I was always uncertain that Baboulis agreed with me. When advertising dollars became scarce during the economic collapse at the end of the Bush Presidency, when all the stations were cutting staff, Baboulis jettisoned Lydia Kulbida. He used the economic downturn to disguise the real reason for her firing, her active support of the union at WNYT. I wrote a newspaper blog describing her termination as the result of her union activity rather than economics. I was also aware that she had resisted what she thought were some heavy handed ownership attempts to inject bias into WNYT reports on ecology and unionization. By that time, I'd retired and no longer had a stake or a say in any decision at Channel 13, but some old friends in management verified my blog's allegations to me privately.

Chapter Nine: Interviews

My worst experience with fear during an interview caused the woman sitting on set to become virtually paralyzed. She was a Ph.D. physicist from the State University at Albany. The topic was supposed to be esoteric anyway, but when she saw herself on a studio monitor she completely froze. She remained almost catatonic for the entire five minutes.

My most successful interview involved my deliberate use of the word "boy" to describe a black man to a black man. I fully understood the risk I took at the time. In that case, I was also trying to overcome the natural fear that many people experience when being exposed so publicly. When interviews were done live, there were not many options for breaking the barrier caused by a sort of terror.

Both experiences occurred on my PBS local newscast "Live at Ten" on WMHT's onetime partner at Channel 45. The program was just 15 minutes in duration but had no commercial breaks. I had no staff, but I did have some support from various interns and part-timers working the "scanner desk" that was part of the Live, Local, Late Breaking format for the 11 o'clock WNYT newscast. My public broadcast channel newscast always ended with a five-minute interview.

The African American man was extremely old. I'd met him just an hour before the live broadcast. His grandfather had been a slave. He had been raised in the Old South, had seen one lynching and knew of many others. He had been raised in a time of real terror, and he had stories that had mesmerized me when we talked in my office. When he couldn't conquer the on-air fear, my question was, "Tell me about the Peterson boy." He did, non-stop for four minutes.

I was concerned about using the word "boy," but he'd used it repeatedly in telling me the story privately. I needed him to relax and forget about being interviewed. I expected viewers might object to me calling a black man a boy, but it relaxed him. I knew he had an interesting story to tell if I could just get him over the fear, and I knew he would react to "Peterson Boy" because that was his word and it triggered a story he had just told, so he remembered it and relaxed. As he left, his caretakers were laughing and said that he'd never talked so much.

The physicist interview couldn't be saved. I wanted to discuss quantum entanglement, which Albert Einstein had called, "spooky action at a distance." There are implications about the nature of reality in the result of actual experiments with a mathematical relationship that were discovered by an Irish physicist named John Bell. It's a topic that fascinates me and about which I've done a lot of reading. So, I wound up trying to describe the implications while my guest could manage only an occasional nod. The interview was a disaster.

Then there was the guy who told me, "I'll go wherever General Burgoyne sends me." That was just more funny than disastrous. I was forced to answer, "That's fine, but you're fighting for General Gates."

Again, fear had gripped a guest who'd been composed and articulate just minutes before. He was one of two guests on that program in September of 1992. Both were Revolutionary War re-enactors who had come to the studio to help plug a commemorative event on the Saratoga Battlefield. I was able to loosen up both of them a bit by joking and teasing them.

Laughter almost always works to unfreeze a terrorized interviewee, but how do you get them to laugh? I found a method that I'm sure I used hundreds of times, almost always on males only, but it only works for recorded interviews. All that is required is the ability to maintain an unflinchingly serious poker face after asking, "When, sir, did you last get laid?" Point the microphone toward the interview subject and just wait. Every time, without exception, the nervous subject eventually exploded in laughter. Sometimes, people started to answer before concluding that the question had to be bogus.

Politicians were experienced at being interviewed, so ice-breaking was never an issue in any interview with a public figure. Instead, veracity was the difficulty with them. All journalists deal with on the record information as a default status. Off the record information must be given that status in advance. The problem arises when the person being interviewed assumes off-camera is off-record, which it most definitely is not. A very common problem of that type arose in my last live interview with former Congressman John Sweeney.

I'd known him for years, way back to his youthful days in Rensselaer County politics. He eventually was beaten by Kirsten Gillibrand in 2006. In

2000, he was in Florida after his first reelection working to get Florida's electors into the column of President George W. Bush during a viciously contested recount of the election there. Sweeney's effort to force a decision for Bush saw him identified as a "thug" by Harvard Professor Alan Dershowitz, who identified him by name on national television several times as a leader of the rowdies in the Florida recount. (Ultimately, the entire issue was resolved with a U.S. Supreme Court decision that put Bush back into the White House even though his opponent, former Vice President Al Gore, had beaten Bush in the national popular vote by 500,000.)

Two years later, after another re-election, Sweeney was in the studio of WNYT for a live interview. The station had added a segment to the 5:30 newscast in which I routinely interviewed news makers. Before the Sweeney segment, the congressman was telling me how his influence on the Hill had slipped with the election of a larger GOP majority. He was a Northeast Republican in the House of Representatives and felt he had more sway when the GOP majority was slim. When the party no longer really needed his vote, he told me, its leaders were less inclined to court the moderates from the Northeast.

That was news that my viewers should know, I concluded. When I asked him on air whether an increased GOP majority would reduce his influence, he ridiculed the question as being about something people always talk about but which is never true. He just flat out lied about something he'd told me just minutes before. It was a common practice.

So common, in fact, that it's possible for an experienced journalist finally to decide not to listen to any more political lies. That happened to me on the night the Supreme Court of the United States decided that George W. Bush had won the 2000 Presidential election. Two congressmen were in studio for a late news broadcast and were interviewed by me. Sweeney was joined by Democrat Mike McNulty. Both were handing me a bunch of nonsense about pulling together and uniting behind Bush.

I interrupted and said to McNulty, "Oh really? Does that mean you are going to support Bush's tax cuts?"

"Hell, no," was the answer.

I turned to Sweeney and said, "You were called a thug for leading the so-called Brooks Brothers riot in Florida. Do you think liberal activists are going to forget that in a hurry?" He was insulted by the question.

The interview became contentious. The harmony theme was shattered, and some people went bonkers over what I'd done. The right-wing radio talkers, the e-mailers and the phone callers were livid. How unpatriotic of me to smash the illusion of a united nation going forward.

Of course, I knew better. If I hadn't been exhausted and in horrible pain, I might not have broken the rules. It can be disastrous for a television news anchor to tell people what they don't want to hear. I knew better.

Howard Tupper, Ernie Tetrault, Ed Dague and Bob MacNamara

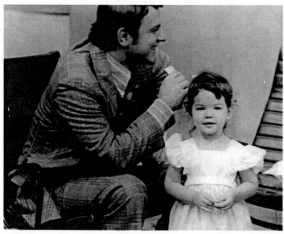

Ed with daughter Becca

Hito's last weather show, 1978
From left: Jim Delmonico, Jan Tupper, Howard Tupper, Ed Dague

City Hall Greeting

The Knickerbocker News Photo by Bob Paley

A sober-faced Mayor Corning is besieged by newsmen as he arrives at Albany City Hall today, following an announcement yesterday that students were to march on City Hall in protest of the police action in yesterday's violence at Albany High School. Students from State University in Albany gathered at the City Hall, then were scheduled to march on the Public Safety Building, where those arrested yesterday were to be arraigned.

With Bill Cosby and Chris Kapostasy

At Albany School of Humanities, 1993

Interviewing Paul Tonko

Chapter Ten: The Lambdin Incident

On a Friday evening in May of 1984, I returned to the WRGB newsroom after my dinner break and found the late news producer particularly happy to see me.

"Oh, great, you're here," Donna Evans said to me as she handed me the telephone. "It's Bill Lambdin from Channel 13, and I don't know how to handle his announcement."

Lambdin was the leader of the NABET union at WNYT. It was the same union that had been on strike against WRGB for the preceding two weeks. Lambdin was calling with a news release, which he was reading without taking questions.

A contract settlement had been reached between WNYT–NewsChannel 13's then-owner, Viacom Inc ., and the very same NABET union that was striking Channel 6. The press release Lambdin read contained mostly explicit criticism of the new owners of WRGB, a leverage buyout specialty firm on Wall Street named Forstmann, Little and Company.

The Channel 6 strike was blowing WRGB apart. Tensions inside WRGB were so high that I understood the producer handing me the Lambdin problem. Lambdin was calling WRGB's proprietors greedy absentee owners interested only in bleeding WRGB to pay their debt. His comments were easily the most incendiary made by anyone since the strike had begun. And he was calling us so we could put his comments on the air.

We could have just chucked the story and ignored it, but then we'd have been guilty of suppressing news to protect the owners of the station we worked for. Instead, I wrote the story as fairly and honestly as I could. I tried to pretend I was writing it somewhere else and gave the WNYT settlement just the usual 20-second copy story. Some of Lambdin's comments were included because they constituted most of his release. But, like producer Evans, I wasn't about to take responsibility for putting it on air.

I called News-Director Don Decker at home and explained my problem. The Lambdin statement was written up as a story, and I wanted him to hear it before it ran.

"I can't hear it," Decker said. "I'm sure you did your best, and good luck."

Click! Decker had hung up on me.

I was stunned and told the newsroom what had happened. Now, finding myself rather amazed by this turn of events, I called the operations manager, Charlie King. I explained what had just happened with Decker. I wanted King to hear the story before I read it on air.

King told me that he fully understood Decker's refusal to listen to the story and that he, too, did not dare hear it. Then he went further and talked off-the-record. He said that general manager Jim Delmonico was out of control over the strike and that no one could predict his next move. King told me that he and Decker had sat in Delmonico's office every morning on the edge of their seats listening to what they viewed as irrational rants and threats. He wished me the best of luck with the story and hung up. So, it ran as I had written it, and I read it on air without much expression. The worst week I'd experienced in a long time was over. I went home for the weekend.

Donna Evans was working a fast turn-around on the assignment desk the following morning, Saturday. She called me at home in early afternoon. In a hushed whisper, she said she wanted me to know that Delmonico was storming through the television station vowing to fire me. It was the Lambdin piece that had set Delmonico off, of course. I dreaded my return to WRGB on Monday.

Nonetheless, I was there earlier than scheduled, as usual. I'd been called in to cover a story. Decker called me into his office and told me that he had cooled off Delmonico and saved my job. He said that he'd put the Schenectady Gazette's newspaper report on Bill Lambdin on Delmonico's desk next to my script and showed Delmonico that the reports were almost identical. Decker never mentioned hanging up on me and refusing to listen to the story.

I saw Delmonico several times in the newsroom, and he avoided talking to me. In fact, he made quite a show out of it. I wonder if he ever considered how I might react. He seemed to be totally surprised when I quit.

Chapter Eleven: Laughter and the News

It may have been the most devilish thing I've ever done. A man I liked, a colleague worrying about his job, turned to me for advice. I set him up for a fall so huge that he might have been fired on the spot. I just couldn't resist.

Ernie Tetrault, the primary news anchor at WRGB for over a decade, had a problem. The hour-long 6 O'clock newscast was tough to fill with real news, so a regular time filler was created and broadcast weekly. Every Thursday evening at about 6:50 PM, Channel Six broadcast a summary of upcoming artistic events. It filled four or five minutes with some of the most boring stuff in broadcast history. It was so bad that it was sometimes funny -- at least to the people on set, if not to the management.

Management became increasingly aware that the broadcasters found it humorous. Maybe the fact that every week the anchor who tried to introduce the report broke out laughing was a clue. Maybe the loud snoring sound that accompanied the introduction --as the Sports reporter, Bob McNamara, expressed his opinion of the content -- gave the manager a hint. Whatever it was, the word came down that there had better be no more laughter while introducing "The Arts Calendar."

Tetrault's problem that evening was that the line-up for the newscast indicated that he was the one scheduled to introduce the weekly snorer, and he feared he might get into real trouble if he laughed. He had not yet looked ahead at the scripted introduction when, during the first commercial break, he turned to me for help.

Tetrault said to me, "Ed, I've got the arts calendar lead tonight, and if I laugh Decker will fire me. You thought that jumper story was funny last night, but you got through it without laughing. How did you do that?"

I knew he had the Arts Calendar lead coming up because, unlike Tetrault, I'd read the entire show script. I not only knew that he was scheduled to introduce the piece, I knew exactly what the scripted lead required him to say. That's when the idea popped into my head.

"Well, Ernie," I answered thoughtfully, "I thought of my responsibilities, my wife and kids' future, my mortgage and car notes, and that kept me focused on not laughing. And, besides that," I added, "I was squeezing my left nut hard the whole time."

Tetrault chuckled, and we went on with the newscast. I knew that he sometimes didn't read ahead in the script, but I really didn't expect that he would attempt a cold read on the Arts Calendar introduction. He did, though. So, about 40 minutes after my advice was given, he turned the page and encountered this in the script: "IN THIS WEEK'S ARTS CALENDAR, BILL FORTUNE REPORTS THE NUTCRACKER OPENS SUNDAY AT THE SARATOGA PERFORMING ARTS CENTER."

Tetrault never finished the lead. He got about as far as the word "Sunday" when his eyes suddenly widened, his jaw vibrated a bit, and then his head went straight down on the desk as laughter consumed his entire being. People at home saw about five seconds of him doubled over with his body heaving in laughter before the recorded piece came up on screen.

The next day, he told me, that the boss did indeed call him into the office for a scolding, but Tetrault interrupted and explained what had happened. He told me that he'd walked out of the office with the boss still doubled over laughing, and that ended the discussion.

Laughter can be a real problem on a TV news set because it's a bit like being in church. You're just not allowed to laugh. There can also develop a group dynamic in which one person's laughter can infect an entire news team, including the people running the cameras. It can be very hard to regain control to go on with the show. In the worst cases directors have had to roll unscheduled commercials rather than continue to show a news set filled with hysterical people unable to control themselves.

There are some broadcast legends about laughter-producing events, staged deliberately to break up announcers. Scripts have been set on fire, long cloth-covered tables have been set just out of sight below studio windows so a man in scuba gear could appear to swim by and, according to one story, the penis of a slain moose was once pinned inside a staffer's fly just to generate laughter on the set. I've always preferred more verbal methods.

Once, Tetrault had done a report that was fairly humorous all by itself, but my policy of reading every line of every script in advance allowed me to plan an apparent ad-lib in advance. It was about the potato chip and its original inventor. In Tetrault's report, two women were involved in a dispute over the invention. Mary Lou Whitney, a wealthy woman who dominated the social scene in Saratoga Springs for decades, maintained it was her husband's relative who'd produced the first chip. But a local historian took issue and maintained that the potato chip's creator "was a Chinese cook at the old Blue Moon Inn." There was humor in the report, and Tetrault had written out his closing comment, which was to look like an ad-lib. So, as planned, after his piece ended, he turned to me and said, "At least, Ed, the women agree on something. They should be called Saratoga Chips."

"Well, thank God they weren't invented in Buffalo," I replied, and the entire studio exploded in laughter -- except me, of course. My demeanor remained totally serious.

That serious deportment can make absurd comments funny because it is so contrary to the actual content. Once, when reporting in studio for Benita Zahn's 5:30 newscast at WNYT, I related a story about a plan to open a casino in the Catskills. A Native American tribe had purchased land and was proposing to open the type of operation that was succeeding in various places from Connecticut to the Mohawk Valley.

When I finished, Benita observed that, "This might be able to revive the whole area around it. It could really bring back the old Borsht Belt."

"It might," I replied. Then, with a totally serious demeanor, I added, "although Indians were never really into borsht."

I was almost out of the studio and Zahn had moved onto another story when the absurdity of my totally deadpan observation hit her. She broke out laughing and could not stop. I just kept on walking.

When Lydia Kulbida became co-anchor with me, she was barely situated when I first provoked laughter from her. We'd just finished her first 6 O'clock newscast. Some of her understandable initial nervousness had passed when I announced that I had to pee. She was unaware that we video-taped the early evening, three-second tease segments right after that newscast. I'd been doing it for years, of course, and knew that the scripts dropped on the anchor desk at 6:30 were for those teases. I'd read the script before launching into my, "I've got to pee," drama.

I stamped my feet and said it over and over. I said, "I've got to pee. Oh, my, do I have to pee! Do you know what that's called?"

By this time, I assumed she thought I was deranged, and she simply replied, "No."

"I'll get back to you on that," I said and then just waited for the Teleprompter to be loaded so she could read her first tease. There had been a release of radioactive water at the Indian Point reactor down the Hudson River, so when the taping was set to begin and the teleprompter was loaded, Lydia was confronted with the first tease. It read: "A LEAK ALERT IS ISSUED IN THE AREA. DETAILS AT ELEVEN."

I had to record all three teases that evening, since Lydia was laughing.

At times, I've done that to myself. One morning when I was handling radio newscasts for the highly rated WGY morning show, I was reading UPI wire copy about the previous night's activity along the Suez Canal. It was a totally routine story that a skirmish between Egyptian forces and Israeli commandos had erupted. Egypt reported the loss of two soldiers, a jeep and six camels. The camels did it to me. It was the first and only time I'd encountered a casualty report listing lost animals, and I started to laugh. I could not stop laughing. Every time I tried to move on, I would laugh anew. Finally, I abandoned the attempt and went back to the morning disc-jockey, Bill Edwardsen, only to find that he, too, was laughing.

Sometimes, everyone around you on the news set is laughing, but you dare not succumb to the temptation. My worst experience with that was at WNYT-NewsChannel 13, where I was in the middle of a newscast when a late breaking story was added. At the time, the station had a series of topical briefs called "info segments." They were usually recorded, but if they were written to close to the deadline they had to be done live. That was the case on the evening in question.

The late addition to the newscast concerned word from the Centers for Disease Control in Atlanta that, for the very first time, they'd confirmed a case of AIDS being passed from a woman to a man. Until that time, it had been believed that AIDS transmission went only one way -- from a man to a woman. The late addition was fairly explicit, employing the words penis and vagina – words rarely used in television news. Well, no problem. Nothing funny at all about that.

However, the next words I had to read were: "IN TONIGHT'S HEALTH

INFOSEGMENT, MEN ARE YOU HAVING TROUBLE WITH YOUR JOINTS?"

Instantly, every person in the studio started laughing. Not me. God knows I wanted to, but it was one of those times when it would have been a huge problem, so I got through it with a straight face. Sometimes, laughter is so out of place that the audience really will take offense.

Such was the case one night when I was anchoring a 30-second update in the middle of a network show. It was a single anchor segment, but my co-anchor, Chris Kapostasy, accompanied me to the studio to continue a conversation we'd been having. In those days, the Teleprompter (which is a trademarked name for the device in the way that Xerox is a trade marked name for a copier) was not connected to the output of a computer but to the output of a small camera. Typed scripts on standard letter sized paper were lined up on a conveyor belt and moved beneath the camera.

On this night, there was no operator available to handle the prompter duty. So, Chris said, "I'll run the prompter for you, Ed". I asked her if she had ever run it before. I distinctly recall her saying, "No, but how hard can it be?" She started out doing just fine. But after a few seconds, one of the sheets of paper caught on something and started to rotate and the conveyor belt moved.

On air, I was doing fine. Even when the page started to spin, I was doing fine. I was aware that I was reading a script that, at that instant, was upside down and moving backwards, but I hung in there and continued to be coherent. Until she started banging the machine with a wrench, that is. *Bang! Bang!* I broke out laughing.

I was reading a story about a rape on the SUNY Albany campus when something just broke me up. I got control and apologized, noting to the audience that something in studio had made me laugh, but that didn't matter to some viewers. They called and were livid. I can't say that I blame them. Laughter is a chronic problem for broadcasters. It's an enemy that can come out of nowhere and ruin a broadcast. Or, it can confirm to viewers that an anchor is aware of a mistake having been made.

On election night in November of 1982, long before the polls closed, I was interviewing a candidate on air live. His name was David Roberts, and he would lose his contest for the New York State Assembly that night, but at 7:25

in the evening no one knew that. Actually, the interview was little more than a time filler, but I did have a scrap of information. I'd developed an exit poll for use by WRGB. The poll showed that Mario Cuomo was doing well in the Schenectady area in his race to become governor of New York. I wondered if Cuomo's strength might aid fellow Democrat Roberts.

The question I'd tried to ask was, "Dave, do the governor's exit poll coattails reach as far down as the Assembly race?" Granted, it was a clumsy construction that might have been hard to understand anyway, but what actually came out of my mouth was far worse:

"Dave," I asked solemnly, "do the governor's Kotex reach as far as the Assembly?"

Immediately, in my earpiece, I heard laughter. Upstairs in the control room, producer Bill Duffy had opened the intercom to my earpiece and was screaming, "Hee-hee-hee, you asshole! Do you know what you said?"

I did know what I'd said, but I sat on camera as motionless as a stone unable to decide how to correct it. I finally just let it go, figuring that this guy was a politician used to talking about anything, so let him handle that. Poor Roberts' eyes widened and, he touched the earphone in his right ear. "I don't think I got the question, Ed," he said.

"Well, that's too bad," I had the chutzpah to say, "Let's just move on." The following day when I went to interview Cuomo his state police bodyguard saw me, laughed and asked, "Hey Ed, are you still employed?"

Miraculously, I was.

My guess is that most viewers had probably missed what I'd said. In college, at RPI where the sport of hockey is king, I'd learned that people often hear what was intended rather than what was actually said. In early 1964, during my broadcast of the play by play for the championship hockey game of the Eastern College Athletic Conference, in the midst of my high speed talking trying to describe the high drama of a period of non-stop action, I made the worst mistake of my career. Later, I found that most listeners missed my exact words. My partner, the color commentator, slid off his chair laughing at my mis-speak, and I certainly knew what I'd said. Most hockey fans, though, seemed to have heard my intended call rather than my actual one, which was:

"R-P-I breaks out of the zone. Brinkworth pisses across ice to Knightly … who shits … on goal … but the fuck is cleared into the corner."

Chapter Twelve: Celebrity

The site was an Albany area eatery named Platt's Place. The time was sometime in the late 1970s. A guy stood near the front door and pointed toward me as I was sitting with my family at the back of the room. It was amazing because he didn't move at all; he just stood pointing for a ridiculously long period of time. After a few minutes, it became bothersome, as other patrons started to look for his target.

After about 15 minutes of this guy holding his point like a hunting dog, the stunt began to unnerve my son, daughter, wife and even me, despite my familiarity with the reactions of some people to coming across somebody they see on television. It was one of my worst experiences with the celebrity problem so familiar to people in TV news. The episode proved to be so unsettling that we finally just abandoned our meal and left. That was a memorable incident, but there were hundreds of others over the decades when I was on television.

There was an interesting theory advanced by visiting TV consultants about celebrity in the area. Albany is a medium-sized market, roughly a million people out of a nation of 310 or so million, and has no major league sports team, no top level professional theater and no other venues capable of routinely producing area celebrities -- except the local television stations. The consultants told me that few people in areas aside from medium markets like Albany consider local television anchors to be major celebrities.

Fame has driven television performers I've known to change careers. The prime example was Herb Stevens, who was the meteorologist when I started at WNYT in 1984. He was a dedicated forecaster who had worked for the Weather Channel, broadcasting from Atlanta, before being hired by Channel 13. He had nationwide exposure in that job, but he told me that the recognition he got with a national audience was nothing like what he experienced in Albany. It upset him so much that he confided to the station managers that he could not tolerate it much longer, and they replaced him.

Stevens found it difficult to be recognized wherever he went. Most people simply stare. Some point. Too many decide they want a personal meeting. Most of those are well-meaning fans who want to express appreciation for the performer's work. Not all are polite, however. In an Italian restaurant one evening when my wife and I were trying to celebrate our anniversary quietly, a man approached our table to ask if I was Ed Dague. When I said yes, his answer was, "I just wanted to tell you that I hate your fucking guts."

There's nothing that any celebrity performer can do about that type of behavior. If I'd confronted the man in the restaurant, I would have achieved nothing except perhaps convincing other diners that I was arrogant or overly sensitive. I so often heard from people how this anchor or that reporter had been uncivil to a fan who merely wanted to say hello. I'm sure that others said the same about me even though I made a point of trying to be pleasant to every greeter. At times, though, I may have been in a hurry and cut someone off short. Often I was in pain and not able to smile and fake being cordial.

Eventually, like most of the other television performers I knew, I became a bit of a recluse. It was virtually impossible to go to a big shopping mall. I still recall Bob McNamara's unwillingness in a discussion we had on set one evening to believe that I would even try shopping at a mall. Chris Kapostasy used to joke about going out in disguise -- always wearing a hat and sunglasses, at least. That could be effective until people heard me speak and recognized my voice. One day, when Donna and I were ordering lunch at a restaurant, the waitress reacted strongly to my voice. She said that she used to hear it coming from her parents' room so often when she was a child. I'd never thought of that before.

Only once did I really turn on a person who recognized me and made an unpleasant comment. My reaction stunned her into thinking about her comment and finally apologizing for it. My back pain was extreme after sitting in bleachers at my son's school event, and I took my family out afterward for dinner. As I walked by a table, a woman said, "Ed Dague. If you get any wider, I'm going to have to buy a second television to see all of you."

I stopped and said to her, "Why do you feel free to say that to me? You don't know me. You wouldn't say that to a friend of yours. You wouldn't say that to any stranger you meet, so why do you feel free to say something like that to me?"

I recall my wife and kids being astonished. They'd never seen me turn on someone in public. Being a celebrity greatly complicated my life and could become a burden to my whole family.

The celebrity factor also was a journalistic complication that limited my ability to cover stories. It proved to be very difficult for a long-tenured main news anchor to cover a routine story without becoming a distraction. The well known celebrity's presence at a routine meeting could change the whole nature of the event. That probably had something to do with my fondness for reporting on national political conventions or the New Hampshire primary -- or almost any story taking place out of the immediate area where my celebrity was not a factor.

There were also some benefits, of course. The news staff understood that I might get through on the telephone to someone who was ducking calls from lesser known reporters. That was an asset we sometimes utilized. In 1993, I was in Boston to cover the final NBC broadcast of new episodes of *Cheers* -- a sensationally successful situation comedy --- and decided to interview some Albany area people who were there for the celebration. My cameraman asked me, "How are we going to find local people"?

"That's easy," I told him. "Just watch."

I then walked out of the restricted area toward the crowd of people being kept behind the police lines. Immediately, quite a few people yelled, "Hey, Ed". We'd found our interview subjects quickly. Whenever I was working an out-of-town story, I always found my celebrity made it easier to find Albany area people and to hear stories they might not tell any other journalist. It could even help me get on-camera interviews with politicians I'd never met before.

The day after Congressman Hugh Carey won the Democratic party nomination to run for governor of New York State, he arrived in Albany on a private plane, exited it and walked straight toward me saying, "Hello, Ed." I'd never met him before. I'm sure that a staffer looking out the plane window briefed him on who was waiting. Senator Charles Schumer did much the same thing in the U. S. Capitol building before I'd been introduced to him. I got some decent stories because of my celebrity, so fame was not entirely a bad thing.

Celebrity could generate free passes to movies -- if I asked, and I always hated to ask. That actually became a source of some tension between me and colleague Ernie Tetrault at WRGB, who used to gripe that when I paid instead of requesting a freebee I ruined things for other performers -- especially those named Tetrault, I suspect. There was always an inherent danger in accepting special treatment, of course. It could easily lead to allegations of bias and therefore was almost never worth it.

There were some benefits to being a reporter regardless of my celebrity, like easier parking for the press, that I did accept and appreciate. And there were a few instances, like parking at RPI Hockey games, where I sometimes conned attendants into believing there existed special accommodations for the press that didn't really exist.

My son, Harris, was always aware of the benefits he might derive from having a famous father and steadfastly avoided all of them as a matter of principle My daughter, Rebecca, occasionally found creative ways to manipulate her circumstances using her father's celebrity. One evening while I was working at WNYT she hurt her toe in an accident at home and had to visit a busy hospital emergency room. My daughter called me in the newsroom and asked if I would use my clout to get them faster medical treatment. I said I would not.

So, my daughter approached the triage nurse and told her, "My father is at work and he may call to see how I'm doing, and I wanted to tell you that I'll be sitting over there."

The nurse said, "All right, what's his name?"

"Ed Dague," answered my daughter, Rebecca.

She told me the nurse's reaction was, "Your father is Ed Dague? I think we can get you into an examination room right away."

On another occasion, my daughter and I went shopping at an area supermarket. Rebecca usually walked well behind me because she enjoyed watching people's reactions if they recognized me. On this occasion, as I left the market well ahead of my daughter, a woman who was entering stopped, turned and watched me walk across the parking lot to my car. Becca approached the woman and said, "Do you think it's him?"

"Yes," the unknown shopper told this complete stranger next to her. "I think it's Ed Dague."

"Well, I'm going to ask him," replied my daughter and then walked to our car, got in and immediately said, "Dad, look at the expression on the face of the woman in front of the market as we drive by her."

I did. Her mouth was open in astonishment.

The strangest case of recognition probably was one that occurred in Anaheim, California. My wife and I were on vacation and visiting Disneyland when a couple approached us and asked if I was Ed Dague. When I said I was, they started laughing. They were also on vacation and lived in the Schenectady suburb of Scotia. They told us they'd wondered whether they would encounter any celebrities while visiting California, but they had encountered just one -- me.

There's one amusing consideration with regard to TV celebrity that was brought up to one of my mentors. It was a story he used to tell me whenever we had a drink after the late news. His name was Howard Tupper, and he'd worked in broadcasting for so many years that he may have known Marconi. I know that he knew NBC's first chief announcer, Colin Hager, because he introduced me to Hager one night at WRGB. I was impressed.

Tupper's story was about sitting at a table having a beer one night while a man at the bar kept staring at him. Tupper was beginning to get disturbed, and apparently the man realized that because he approached Tupper and apologized. He explained that there was something about celebrities that he had always wanted to know. It really bothered him a lot, and he acknowledged Tupper as being about as recognizable a celebrity as the area had at the time.

"So, what is it that you have wondered for so long," Tupper asked the man.

The man answered, "Where do people like you go to cheat on your wife?"

Chapter Thirteen: Religion and the News

When I started working at WNYT in 1984, I knew that the station had fired anchor Craig Alexander to make way for me to anchor the station's newscasts. I worried at first that Alexander's friends at Channel 13 would resent me for creating the situation that had ended their pal's tenure. Apparently, I needn't have worried.

Just a couple of days after I started there, 6 O'clock producer Leslie Moran explained that to me. She was bright enough to anticipate my concern, so she volunteered some background on Alexander. Her opinion was that he wasn't particularly liked by people in the newsroom for several reasons. One concerned his over-the-top religious beliefs, which had on at least one occasion become too clear to viewers.

Alexander had anchored the newscasts on Christmas Eve and had departed from the script, Moran told me, to air a religious rant. At some point in the newscast, he'd evidently become so enraptured with the evangelical possibilities inherent in his television position that he'd told the viewing audience that they must not forget that the approaching holiday was established to honor his lord and savior. I don't know how long he went on, but it was too long the instant he started it.

He'd also at one time purportedly acted in a most unchristian manner by humiliating former anchor Wilson Hall in the middle of the newsroom. A lot of people at WNYT (and a few outsiders, including me) thought highly of Hall. Alexander's rough characterization of Hall as being an old man in a young person's business did not sit well with the staff.

It wasn't until I went to WNYT that religion ever became a factor in the workplace for me. The general manager who hired me, Don Perry, was so religious that he used to host morning prayers meetings for his staff in his office, I was reliably informed. It was told to me by other managers that Viacom, the owner of the station at the time, heard about his meetings and ordered him to end them. Perry never discussed his religious beliefs with me, and it may not have played a role in our relationship, although he likely knew that I was not a believer.

His religiosity did affect one station performer, however, and in a big way.

Herb Stevens was the meteorologist at WNYT when I began working there. He was a fundamentalist Christian who even believed that the planet Earth was young, based on creationists' arguments. One starry night when he and I had stepped outside, Herb looked at the stars and said, "Just think, Ed, the light from those stars has been traveling for millions of years to reach us."

I replied, "Not in your theology."

Stevens laughed and said, "You're right."

It was a rare opportunity for me to hit someone with a real scientific background with facts that could challenge, if not demolish, his religious beliefs, but I passed. We were pretty close friends by then, and I don't make a habit of demolishing people's beliefs just for fun. Maybe I should have, for those beliefs were going to shorten his tenure at WNYT.

Stevens had a problem with being a celebrity, and we'd talked about it often. There was no simple solution, and he should have known that, but as he grew more uncomfortable with being recognized by the public so frequently he decided to discuss it with another broadcaster known to have strong Christian beliefs, general manager Perry. The day that Stevens stopped by my office to tell me about his plans I tried hard to dissuade him.

"Don is a Christian, but he is a businessman first," I told Stevens.

I tried to warn him that Perry wouldn't be happy knowing that a front line performer was unhappy and would act on that.

"No," Stevens said to me, "I'm just going to talk to him as one Christian to another."

Stevens insisted that the conversation would be no more than a discussion between devout believers with nothing more involved. Stevens decided to ignore my words of caution. Two months later, when Perry told Stevens he'd done him a huge favor and replaced him with Bob Kovachick, Stevens didn't see it as one Christian aiding a fellow Christian but as exactly what it was -- a businessman covering his bases so as not to be caught shorthanded by an unhappy employee.

WNYT was the first station I'd encountered where so many staffers were overtly religious. Elaine Huston, a reporter and anchor of the late afternoon newscast, displayed her Christian beliefs very openly with framed prayers and religious icons on her desk. Sometimes, she talked openly about her beliefs.

Once, while we sat together in the make up room, she told me she was praying that God changed the news director's mind about some issue.

I explained to her that such a thing was impossible because it was contrary to a belief in free will. She answered that she didn't believe in "all that free will stuff." I tried to get her to understand that sin was impossible without free will. She didn't want to hear it, and I never pressed other people on religious beliefs.

My co-anchor and close friend for the 11 years we worked together, Chris Kapostasy, was telling me one Friday night that she and her husband, Robert, were going to be serving as deacons on the alter of her Roman Catholic church that coming Sunday. I usually avoided religious discussions altogether, but on that occasion I asked how she and Bob squared having no children with her church's doctrine on birth control. It was simple, she told me; they just didn't believe that part of Catholic teaching.

I knew from my indoctrination by the nuns in elementary school that the church didn't allow that type of individual decision about doctrinal matters, but I said nothing to her about that. I decided that Kapostasy, like Huston, didn't understand the foundational tenets of their beliefs, as most people do not. I understood only because I'd wrestled with my doubts and dogma for so very long before settling on atheism as my personal philosophy. That was and is still a weak atheism. I think people who are sure there is no god are as deluded as those who are certain that there is.

That personal conclusion was something I absolutely had to hide from viewers for my entire career. In America, any religious persuasion is more acceptable than disbelief. President George W. Bush once asserted that he did not consider atheists capable of being either American citizens or patriots. Fortunately, my religious beliefs never became relevant to my work as a journalist or broadcaster. Yet, there was one slip-up.

A WNYT reporter named Kumi Tucker, a bright and dedicated journalist whose work was always thoughtful, did a series of reports on belief in angels. The series was fine. I had no problem with it, nor did I have any comment on it on air, and that showed enough to some viewers. A number called and left fairly nasty telephone voice mail messages because I'd made no comment on the reality, or lack thereof, of angels. Those viewers had expected me, as the newscast's anchor, to validate their beliefs somehow.

Once though, I did publicly reveal my unease about religious belief and believers. For over a decade, I hosted a public reading by celebrities to raise funds to support a group of volunteers who taught illiterates to read. Many of the beneficiaries of the service were immigrants, and some had reading skills in other languages besides English. It was and remains a worthwhile cause. One year, the organization asked me not just to host their event but to read as well.

I chose Carl Sagan's "The Demon Haunted World" for my reading excerpt and followed with part of Kahlil Gibran's poem "On Children" to make the point that parents who indoctrinate their children with religious nonsense are doing them (and all of mankind) a disservice. Before beginning, I noted the presence of a Christian bishop (not Roman Catholic) in the audience and asked for his tolerance. To my shock, when the event ended, the bishop approached me and thanked me for the reading. He suggested that I would be stunned to know how many established senior clerics agreed with my sentiments.

In recent years, I've become much more aggressive in my objections to religious beliefs because of their intrusion into politics and policy. Particularly disturbing to me is the assertion that anthropogenic climate change is impossible because of religious beliefs. It's bad enough that religion is the basis for the persecution and prosecution of people practicing certain lifestyles, but when it intrudes on my grandchildren's right to live on a habitable planet, I can and have become alarmed.

Chapter Fourteen: Questions and the News

To a very real extent, the anchor of a television newscast is the representative of the viewer. Part of the anchor's job is to ensure that the viewer leaves a broadcast with all reasonable questions about the news answered – or, at the very least, properly addressed.

If something in a story doesn't make sense or if a report leaves an obvious question unanswered, it is the responsibility of the anchor to help the viewer understand. That's part of the reason I followed many live reports with a question to the reporter who'd covered the story. The rest of my reasoning had to do with my belief that viewers prefer some spontaneity in any news broadcast.

At WNYT, I asked a lot of questions of reporters, and they didn't like it. After reporter Chris Brunner left Channel 13 to become news-director of the local Time Warner cable news operation he telephoned me to express his surprise at his own decision to have his anchors question his reporters on air. He also confessed that early in my tenure at WNYT he'd gone to news director Steve Baboulis to ask him to put a end to my after-report questioning. What drove such a dramatic change of mind on Brunner's part?

He'd decided that my questioning had made him a better reporter. He said that I'd made all the reporters sharper because they always had to ask themselves, "What have I missed that Ed will ask?" Other WNYT staffers told me much the same thing. To be honest about it, however, staff development was not the intent of my questioning. My goal was to make the newscast more interesting and understandable to viewers. Making reporters think more about their stories was an additional benefit.

Like everything in life, there were unintended consequences and failures at times. Sometimes I embarrassed reporters. That, most definitely, was not my intent. The worst possible outcome was to force a reporter to say, "I don't know," on air. When that happened, it was generally my fault for asking a stupid question. I also told reporters that sometimes they need not answer because the question itself made the point about the story that I thought needed to be made.

One night, after the dubious arrest of a Lebanese immigrant for a supposed driving violation, information about the legal irregularities involved was given to us off-the-record by a police agency that had no part in the event but was outraged by it. The bogus arrest became horrific when the arrested man had the crap beaten out of him in jail by a guard who was related to the person who'd supposedly been wronged by the driver. After a long discussion about how to get the important, off-the-record perspective into the story, the reporter and I settled on a series of questions. My questions all had to be answered, "We don't know," and those answers made a point that we felt needed to be part of the story.

In that case, there was no embarrassment to the reporter involved. On other occasions, I put a reporter into a position where the answer, "I don't know," was upsetting to the reporter, to me – and, undoubtedly, to viewers as well. Maybe my worst question was asked almost reflexively, and I knew the second it came out of my mouth that it was unreasonable. It involved a report on the continuing hunt for a missing man. A solid reporter named Steve Scoville had been out on the story all day.

The point of the story was that the missing man needed medication. After two days in the Adirondack forest there was real reason to worry about his life. The man was elderly and diabetic, and Scoville's report had included pictures of trackers hacking their way through dense woods accompanied by bloodhounds and hundreds of volunteers. Scoville ended his report with a live stand-up and the observation that, "So far, Ed, all the searchers have been able to find was a gum wrapper."

"Well, he's diabetic. Was it sugarless gum?" I asked and instantly understood that I was asking about a detail the reporter was highly unlikely to know. Scoville didn't know, and he handled it well by noting that he wasn't close to the wrapper when it was discovered. It upset me to have put him in that situation, however. Scoville wasn't happy about it either.

In another case, the embarrassment for the reporter came about because he didn't comprehend my point and, because satellite reports have to be squeezed into a window of time that has no leeway, I had no opportunity to make myself clear. The story was about our hunt for a man who was doing his best to avoid all reporters. Our reporter was one of our best – John Gray, who went on to be the main anchor at the local Fox affiliate. He'd worked a long day, and the incident occurred in the late newscast at 11.

Gray was positioned outside a local hospital with the "EMERGENCY" sign behind him and clearly visible to viewers. Most of the story was on tape. It showed Gray doggedly chasing the man, a public servant with a real duty to comment, as I recall. The pursued man successfully evaded Gray, as the reporter noted in his live stand-up closing. Gray said that the man had finally ducked into the hospital emergency room and added, "They won't let me in."

"They have to let you in," I noted immediately.

I knew the hospital did not have to allow his cameraman inside with all the gear to start shooting pictures, but a hospital emergency room is about as public a place as there is. So, with time getting tight, I chose not to go into detail about his right of access. Instead, I thought I could make the point another way. I said to Gray, "You don't look well." He didn't understand. He took it personally and said, "Well, it's been a long day, and I'm tired". At that moment, the satellite window closed and the report ended.

Gray told me the next day that he'd thrown his microphone on the ground and said to the cameraman, "Why the hell is Dague telling me I don't look good?" Cameraman Lou Swierzowski, Gray told me replied, "John, there is a sign over your shoulder saying 'emergency,' and you're saying they won't let you inside, and Ed was trying to explain that you have to be admitted." Gray told me he'd gone home and asked his wife if she'd seen the show. She said that she had. So, he told me he asked her, "When Ed said I didn't look well, did you understand his point that …" According to Gray later, she'd interrupted and said, "John, everybody understood.".

The problem of absolutely unbending time restrictions on satellite reports caused another type of problem on another newscast. A Schenectady police officer was on trial in federal court in the City of Utica on charges relating to illegal drugs. Our reporter had covered the day's testimony and was ad-libbing his story when the satellite window slammed shut and cut him off. The trouble was that he'd meant to relate to viewers the testimony of a known drug user. As his report was cut off, however, he'd just said that the chief of the Schenectady Police Chief had smoked crack. He'd stated it as a fact.

There was no opportunity to question him, so I reacted by assuring viewers that an allegation of crack use by the chief had been made. My ad-lib effort to attribute the allegation to a witness who was a known drug user was viewed by some people as a defense of the chief. It was an instance where my inability to question a reporter created a situation where we nearly libeled a police official and forced me into an explanation that appeared to some as my defense of the chief. That reporter was never again allowed to broadcast live in an ad-lib situation.

The police chief, incidentally, later went to jail in connection with drug charges.

Chapter Fifteen: Technology

Modern newsrooms depend heavily on computers no matter what medium is used to deliver the finished product. Television newsrooms now have computers handling not just written scripts and prompter displays but also the on-screen graphics and, sometimes, studio camera shots as well. Before computers, early television newsrooms used devices that actually converted kinetic energy in a highly carbonized environment into duplicate copies of symbol-covered paper sheets. In other words, typewriters and carbon paper sets were used to generate scripts.

Most of the typewriters when I started working as a journalist were electric, so they could be set to strike hard. That allowed the fifth copy in a carbon set to be almost legible. The lone exception in the WGY-WRGB newsroom in 1969 was the machine used by sports reporter Bob McNamera. He used an old mechanical typewriter until the mid-'80s because he disliked the electrified ones. We all used to wonder what he would do on the day that a computer keyboard replaced his mechanical relic. Surprisingly, he adapted more quickly than anyone had thought possible. Eventually, McNamara told me that he never wanted to work without a computer ever again.

So much technology was developed during my 40 years in broadcast journalism that almost every aspect of the job was affected. Almost every aspect was made easier, but the essential essence of reporting may be immune to technological change. At its heart, reporting is story telling. The tools to tell those stories have evolved, but a reporter still must present and interest another person in a story told with accuracy and meaning. In short, whatever the technology involved, reporting still involves a level of human artistic talent.

For broadcasters, the first requirement, I've long believed, is the ability to read out loud with comprehension. That means emphasizing some words more than others along with controlling voice pitch and the speed of delivery to convey meaning to the listener. Those skills can be extremely difficult for some people to master. Technology can assist by recording spoken segments to be reviewed and retried. The meaning of a spoken sentence is not merely in the words themselves but also in the way those words are spoken.

On October 20, 1973, I deliberately demonstrated that fact at the end of the weekend newscast I anchored. The events of that night became known as the "Saturday Night Massacre," when America's entire system of constitutional justice was shaken. The President, Richard Nixon, had ordered the U. S. attorney general to fire a special prosecutor who was probing the Watergate affair. The attorney general had refused to carry out that order. Nixon had fired his attorney general and given the same order to the next in command in the U.S. Justice Department. That official also refused to obey and resigned. Finally, the third-ranking official in the justice department followed the order and fired Special Watergate Prosecutor Archibald Cox.

I ended the newscast with a sentence that was a promotional announcement the first time I said it and an editorial when I said it the second time. The sentence was: "Stay tuned for a special report on tonight's developments in Washington to be followed by our regularly scheduled horror show."

My second reading emphasized the words "regularly scheduled" to convey the implication that the special report was also a horror show but one that had not been scheduled. That is a non-technological aspect of the news anchor job. On that cold October night in 1973, I had to memorize the sentence. Today, I could read it off a Teleprompter. That is an area where technology can make the job easier, but it requires a human being to alter the sentence's meaning without changing even a single word.

Advancing technology has revolutionized many peripheral aspects of TV journalism while leaving some essential human aspects unchanged. However, by decreasing some of the stress involved in television performances, technology also has made the human role a bit easier. The biggest technical transformation in broadcast journalism was made by the computer.

Computers replaced more than the typewriters. Gone with typewriters are teletypes, which were little more than remote controlled typewriters that clanged and banged all the time so loudly that they were usually confined to a soundproof booth near the newsroom. The teletypes held rolls of paper and produced yards of printed material all day long. It was news assembled by journalists working for United Press, Associated Press, Reuters, International News Service and other operations, including the national broadcast network with which the station was affiliated. Now, all that is sent directly to a computer to be sorted, filed and displayed as wanted.

The teletypes from the major services had a bell that the machine could ring to signal important breaking stories. An experienced editor could count the number of bells rung almost subconsciously and react only when four or five bell strikes sounded. Three bells rang all the time for stories labeled as "urgent." Four bells could mean something big was breaking -- a bulletin. Five or six bells could break any editor's reverie, as that signaled that a huge breaking story, a flash, was crossing the wires. Occasionally, five bells sounded because a message about an upcoming feature story that the wire service wanted to promote was being printed.

The advent of newsroom computers added new speed and flexibility for television news operations. With computers now receiving the wire service reports and also displaying scripts on the teleprompter, it became possible to move a breaking story directly from the wire services to the Teleprompter in studio without ever printing a copy. It also allowed television producers to amend scripts seconds before they were read. That could be a problem, of course, when it forced television performers to read aloud stories never previewed by them.

My familiarity with computers and with computer programming allowed me to make WNYT's newscasts more current soon after I moved to the station as news anchor and, more importantly in this context, the station's managing editor. I'd studied computer design and several programming languages as an electrical engineering major at RPI. My first program for newsroom use was written while I was at WRGB and was intended for use on election night.

It was written in a language called BASIC on a really early computer called the TI-99 4A, made by Texas Instruments. My program generated a bar graph display of election results from a contested race. The program then had the bars explode and reform to show the results of the next contested election. It was never used on air because we couldn't directly connect the display to the station's video, and our attempt to have a camera take a shot of my monitor produced a washed out appearance. That was disappointing because I'd put a lot of time (my own at home) into writing that program.

At WNYT, I wanted to speed up the process of revising a newscast line-up. When I started working at the station, newscast line-ups were done on a typewriter. It could take a half hour or more to retype a show format and then type a new list of video tapes in the exact order needed for the newly revised newscast. Before commercially written programs for newsroom computer networks were available, I wrote a program for the MS-DOS PC that provided the producer with the ability to revise a newscast layout simply and quickly on a computer screen and then have a printer spit out the "tape list" in seconds. That program allowed us to change our newscasts much closer to airtime than we'd been willing to risk using the manual procedures. That meant that late-breaking stories could be added fairly easily.

That program was written in a language named "Pascal," and it was used to format every WNYT newscast for almost two years before a commercial computer network system named "Newstar" became available. There were copies of my program available on line at one time. It was called "The 30 Minute News," and we put it up without copyright for any journalism school to use.

During the first war with Iraq in 1991, I was able to program the Newstar system to flag every story that mentioned any military unit that included Albany area residents whose name had been registered with us by relatives. WNYT's "Global Search," as we called it on air, allowed the station to track local military and to better connect with the community. It worked so well that a few viewers informed us that they'd reported the station to the Pentagon for revealing unit locations. Since we were scanning and flagging only wire service and network reports, all of our information was gathered from the public domain.

The only technological progress that changed the basic nature of a TV reporter's job, I think, was in the cameras used in the field. The TV news photographer with a shoulder camera is pretty standard now. That wasn't the case when I first started in the business. The first sound camera that was small enough and light enough to be carried so easily was called the CP-16, and the company that made it had been founded in 1968. Before that, the typical sound camera was big and heavy and could be shoulder carried only by someone the size of Sasquatch.

News photographers used two cameras when I first started in the business in 1969. One was necessarily tripod mounted and could shoot sound on film. The other was a small, silent film wind-up camera about the size of today's hand held camcorders. That meant that today's common walking interviews couldn't be done by our local stations and all crowd shots or street scenes were shot MOS. MOS, believe it or not, is a term still used sometimes. It stands for "Mit Out Sound,"

My first television reports were shot on black and white film that was developed as a negative. It was quicker to develop it that way and was electronically inverted to a positive picture during the broadcast. I hated trying to cut film that was always negative pictures. It was viewed on a four-by-three-inch screen in the editing room. What was captured by my photographer was often a mystery to me until it aired. And that wasn't the only difficulty.

If you've ever seen a film projector, you've probably noticed that the pictures are shown as they pass by the lens, but the sound is picked up beneath the lens. That means that the sound is not put on the film where the picture is located, and that has to be considered when editing a news piece. If that distance between sound and picture is ignored, an interviewee's lips start moving before you can hear any words being spoken. We called that effect "lip flap," and it was to be avoided whenever possible.

When color film finally arrived at WRGB in the late 1970's, it was easier to see during the editing of a story, but the lip flap problem was still there. So, in the early 1980s, when video tape technology finally arrived, I was thrilled to see it, sometimes. The early tape cameras were heavy and had to be connected to a heavy recorder. That really disappointed me because my favorite photographer and closest friend in the newsroom, Ken Comstock, could not carry the heavy gear and had to retire on disability.

That was too bad because within a few years technology advanced and the tape cameras grew smaller and lighter. That trend continues today, of course, and it is changing the business in many ways. Reporters can now carry the camera gear in a pocket. As a result, reporters are increasingly being asked to produce reports with video they've shot themselves. Lights are still fairly heavy, but technology has made today's small, lightweight cameras more sensitive, so they require less bright light to produce an air-worthy image. So, again, it's increasingly possible to send a reporter out alone to produce a television news report.

The advances in microwave and satellite technology put more and more emphasis on a reporter's ability to speak extemporaneously. Many established broadcasters were frightened to perform on television without a written script. They found live broadcasting to be intimidating. The rapid advances in live technology forced some out of the business. An ability to ad-lib gradually became a requirement for all news broadcasters. That was one of my strengths from the start of my career. However, in a broadcast from Buffalo in the year 2000, I encountered the most challenging ad-lib circumstance imaginable.

The event was a political debate between Hillary Rodham Clinton and Rick Lazio in the race for the U. S. Senate. It was staged at the PBS station, and one of my jobs was to introduce the moderator, the late NBC correspondent Tim Russert. Essentially, I was filling the time between the end of an NBC sitcom and the beginning of the PBS broadcast. What made it astonishingly difficult was that no one knew how much time I had to fill. My earpiece was connected to the WNYT Producer in Albany, Rick Kissane. He would watch the feed from PBS in Buffalo and feed times cues to me in an effort to make our join-up with PBS seamless.

As I began, no one knew whether I'd be filling 30 seconds or three minutes. So, I had to extemporaneously construct an introduction that was liable to be terminated on 10 seconds notice at any moment, but which also might have to run two or three minutes. The timing depended completely on conditions inside the Buffalo studio. All the notice they could give anyone would be 30 seconds. So, I began by summarizing the careers of the two candidates with no idea of how detailed I should be. All the while, I had to keep track of what I was saying, have a plan for what I'd detail next and have a way to smoothly transition to the moderator.

The first time cue I got from Kissane came about 40 seconds after I started. You can imagine how relieved I was when I heard him say, "Thirty seconds," into my earpiece. From there it was fairly easy because my plan was to move from the candidate's history to Tim Russsert's. In the end, it was a perfectly clean join-up. The cameraman, whom we'd borrowed from WGR-TV in Buffalo, yelled, "Wow, that was clean," That was just what I'd wanted to hear.

After the debate ended, I had to moderate a discussion about it among a panel of people in the Albany studio – people I could not see from my perch in Buffalo. By that point, however, pretending to talk to or interview people as if I could see them when I could not was old hat to me. It was a wrinkle added to the business of news broadcasting by new technology. It's a small wrinkle, and bigger ones are sure to come as technology continues to advance.

It may be that discarded practices will return. Maybe technological advances will generate a new need for new heavy and complex equipment to cover news. It doesn't seem that HD (high-definition television) will force that, but the new trend toward three dimensional television might. If that doesn't bring back a need for multi-person television news crews then maybe hologram TV will. Technological innovations will likely keep the business of broadcast journalism forever changing.

Televisions and computers are clearly merging, and the future of the mechanics of the delivery of news is difficult to imagine. All kinds of circumstances will change, but the basic need for good storytelling will not. News broadcasting looks a lot different today, but I think the basic job being done by television journalists is the same as it was when I started my job in 1969. It's still story telling on a personal basis. It's one person conveying a story to another using a medium that is inherently more personal than printed text can ever be.

Chapter Sixteen: Something Is Up – UFOs

I've experienced four curious incidents over the years involving strange, mysterious objects in our skies. Only one clearly demonstrated a perplexing government secrecy on the topic. The first two were merely unexplained dots of light in the night sky. The third was a story I was working that was quashed, and the outcome of the final incident was so clear that I can't get it out of my mind.

In 1955, a group of boy scouts in my neighborhood, including me, were sleeping outside under the stars in the back yard of one of the boys. As the hour grew late, we stopped talking. I was lying awake in my sleeping bag just gazing up at the stars. After 10 or 15 minutes, I spotted a dot of light moving across the sky from the north to a position directly overhead. There, it seemed to circle another point of light that I'd taken to be a star. Then both lights moved off in a northerly direction. I was amazed, since what I'd witnessed appeared to be a rendezvous of some sort.

One of the boys said, "Did anyone else see that?"

It turned out that everyone in the yard had been lying quietly, looking skyward, and had seen what I'd seen. We discussed it and agreed that we all had watched the same thing. As UFO sightings go, it was meaningless. We saw no ships or structures, just points of light that could not be identified as anything more than that. But the actions of those points of light had seemed deliberate and intelligent.

My second sighting was even flimsier. While walking a girlfriend to her dormitory in 1964, I commented to her on two bright lights on either side of a full moon. I knew they were not celestial objects, since no stars of that magnitude or planets could be so positioned. Five minutes later, as I walked away from the dorm, I noted that the bright points or light were gone but that two jet airplane contrails were visible exactly where the bright lights had been minutes before. I found it all very odd and found it hard to believe that commercial airliners could have made the contrails so close together so quickly.

The third incident was much more detailed. Air traffic controllers at the Albany International Airport tower contacted me about an incident that had taken place several weeks before. New York State Police had called the airport tower, asking the controllers to check their radar. The state troopers were near Round Lake in southern Saratoga County. They were seeing lighted orbs in the sky over their heads. The police reported seeing two orbs that sometimes merged into a single light.

The air traffic controllers told me that they saw strange radar returns on their scopes. Sometimes, they said, there seemed to be three objects reflecting radar emissions, and they occasionally combined into two or even one object. The controllers also told me that a privately owned single engine light plane had been aloft at the time. The controllers had asked the pilot to fly over the lake area and report on any objects in the night sky.

The light plane pilot, they told me, had seen nothing in the air but could see the state police cruisers on the ground with their emergency lights on. The police told the controllers that they could see the small plane directly above the orbs and were amazed that the pilot saw no airborne objects. Eventually, the small plane had to leave the area because of dwindling fuel. The orbs disappeared, they said, and the two state troopers, whose names they provided me, thanked the controllers for their time and the incident ended – well, almost ended.

About half an hour later, the two controllers told me, a U. S. Air Force interceptor out of the Plattsburgh Air Force base contacted the Albany tower requesting permission to come down in altitude to pursue an unknown object heading due north at great speed that had passed under the jet fighter. Having commercial traffic in the area at the time, the air traffic controllers in Albany denied the Air Force pilot's request, but the controllers checked their own radar. They told me that they'd had a clear return from an unknown, airborne object heading north at a speed faster than they could compute from the return. That was the end of their story.

They talked on camera in the tower, and it was a solid interview. It needed some confirmation, so when I returned to WRGB I called the state police substation in Malta, where Round Lake is located, and asked for either one of the state troopers identified by the controllers. Almost immediately, I was connected to the state police major in charge of Troop G at headquarters in the Albany suburb of Loudonville. Shocked, I told him there must have been a mistake, as I was trying to reach two troopers at the Malta substation miles north of him.

"No mistake," he said. "Why do you want to talk to them?"

"About the incident over Round Lake in April," I explained.

The major told me, "They are not allowed to talk about that."

"Okay," I replied. "Who gave that order?"

"I am not allowed to talk about that," the major answered and hung up on me.

That abrupt termination of the telephone call was highly unusual. It's the only time I can recall being hung up on by the state police, much less by a troop commander. Those guys are generally very smooth and do not hang up on television reporters. Then, minutes later, the air traffic controllers called me at the station and told me they were in deep trouble and that I couldn't use their interview clips. If I did, they said, they would have to deny the whole story and claim that they'd only been pulling my leg.

I had no choice. There was no story left, and nothing about it was reported by me that day. Nonetheless, something was seen over Round Lake by responsible police authorities, and that's interesting. More significant is the obvious and successful effort to kill the story by someone in government capable of giving orders to a New York State Police troop commander.

The last incident occurred almost 30 years later, in April of 2004, after my retirement. I was swimming in an indoor therapeutic pool in my home, and a reflection of sunlight, a brief glint of bright light from the sky outside, caught my attention. It was a beautiful, sunny spring day. I moved to the window to see what had reflected the sun so dramatically. I thought I might see a helicopter with a Plexiglas bubble canopy. Instead I saw a doughnut-shaped object moving due east across Saratoga Lake. It seemed to be nearly the color of the sky. I saw it for just a few seconds. It was larger than any aircraft I've seen over the lake and was lost fairly quickly in the trees.

The incident left me absolutely dumbfounded. I had time to realize that what I was seeing was out of place and that I'd never seen anything like it. It seemed to be made of a shiny solid material like Plexiglas and had no light source of its own. I saw no windows, markings or strangeness about it. It struck me as a manufactured flying machine, and it was several seconds after it went out of sight before I realized how marvelously smooth its flight had seemed.

No one else saw it, as far as I know. It certainly seemed real to me, but one of my best friends, a physician, spent some time trying to convince me that I'd experienced an hallucination. That could be the case, but if so, it was the first and only one I've had. The object did not match my conception of a flying saucer. It was round but not saucer shaped. It had no wings and no visible means of propulsion.

I've been unable to forget the incident. I want to know what I saw as I want to know who told the state police major to keep quiet about what his officers had seen.

Chapter Seventeen: Pain

On a November morning in the late 1970s, I awakened in bed, lying on my back, and discovered that I couldn't move. Any attempt to raise my head or to roll onto my side produced a pain in my chest so severe that I was frozen in place. The sharp pain was dead center in my chest, in my sternum. After about 10 minutes marked by repeated episodes of stabbing pain that halted my every attempt to rise, I began to fear being pinned there for hours until my wife returned home.

At long last, I exhaled very deeply, trying to flex my chest. I then felt and heard something snap near the center of my ribs. I then was able to raise my head and to get up without feeling a lot more pain. I did not consider consulting a physician about the incident. It was the sort of thing I'd been living with for much of my life. I attributed that instance to the fact that I'd worked dozens of hours at home in the preceding days, writing an election night broadcast script. I'd experienced considerable chest pain in past years after having spent hours holding my arms in position to type.

Experience had taught me that it was unlikely that any medical practitioner would have an explanation for what had happened to me -- much less a cure. Therefore, it didn't seem to be worth a trip to a doctor's office. Decades later, an expert on my rather uncommon disease, Ankylosing Spondylitis, told me that painful breathing is considered a classic complaint associated with it.

Most of my joints make noises when in motion and have audibly clicked or popped since I was a pre-teen. Only in recent years have I understood what causes it. Swollen muscles, ligaments, and other soft tissues evidently snag on calcium deposits and then noisily snap free. It's not a good thing, and I know that the sounds often are followed by pain in the area of the noise. However, the sound tells me that there also has been an easing of tension in the area and, so I sometimes deliberately manipulate a joint to crack it. When I do that I usually experience a brief release from some of the discomfort.

In 2009, I was able to watch my shoulder bones being scraped of the calcium deposits in much the way a car window is cleared of winter ice. My shoulder joint's insides were displayed on a big high-definition television screen right in front of me as the surgeon scoped the bone and found the blood-red cut-line that was being engraved into my rotator cuff. It was fascinating to watch as he flipped through on-screen menus that popped up to select tools available on the scope. He told me afterwards that the bleeding episode I watched would have ended the procedure a few years ago, before the development of a cauterizing tool for the business end of the Arthroscope.

The speed with which my shoulder regained full movement seemed to astonish the surgeon and the physical therapist who treat me every week. It so amazed them that the therapist joked about wanting a signed affidavit from the surgeon that the operation had really been performed. The nurses at Albany Medical Center were terrific, but they were taken aback a bit by the fact that I could not be given any pain medication after the surgery. My daily dose of methadone had to be sufficient. My ability to tolerate pain has impressed many medical and dental professionals. The physician who first correctly diagnosed my disease predicted that pain tolerance would develop as my nerves tired from the constant pain messaging.

It's all part of my disease; actually an odd family variant of Ankylosing Spondylitis. AS is a type of rheumatoid arthritis that attacks the body's spinal column. The disease generally doesn't strike successive generations, but mine has. AS strikes more men than women, but my sister has a variant of it. My family's version affects joints that are rarely attacked by the disease. My brother was first diagnosed with reactive arthritis and my sister with psoriatic arthritis.

My condition went untreated for decades because U. S. Army physicians and family doctors misdiagnosed it as Spondylolisthesis, which is a displacement of a vertebra rather than a type of arthritis. I understood later that a correct diagnosis would have resulted in avoiding some of the damage done over the decades. Even regular large doses of aspirin apparently would have limited some of the damage caused by the swelling of my joints.

The disease is progressive and continues past early middle age in just 5 per cent of those afflicted, according to some statistics. It's still quite active in all members of my family who are over age 60, including me. It has been inflaming my joints for as long as I can remember. The initial incorrect diagnosis was based solely on the severe back pain that was a common experience for me in my 20s. When my neck became heavily involved in my late 30s, physicians were finally able to correctly identify the affliction. By then, my knees, ankles, hips and shoulders had been involved for years. I think it started in my wrists, because pain and a grinding noise began for me in elementary school. Then the pain moved up my arm, and I vividly recall learning how to ease shoulder tension by snapping something in my elbow joints during the summer of 1965.

While working as a street reporter for WRGB, essentially 1971 to 1984, I experienced some terrible backaches that lingered for weeks. Those had been predicted by the doctors who'd made the incorrect diagnosis, so the pain seemed to confirm their finding. I continued believing that the cause was a congenital deformity involving the incompletion of a fusion of bones in my back. There was a surgical correction available, but the success rate was so low that no personal physician of mine ever considered it an advisable risk. I used to take over-the-counter pain killers only, and I tried some muscle relaxing prescription drugs with some success.

Doctor Marvin Humphrey of Schenectady was my physician for more than a decade. He was an astoundingly good diagnostician. The specialists were stunned that Humphrey was able to tell me that I had Ankylosing Spondylitis following a brief office examination -- no blood test, no radiographs, just an examination of my neck after I complained of constant stiffness. That was all he had, and he nailed the cause and sent me off to the Albany Medical College's rheumatology professor. The specialist tried a lot of drugs to reduce inflammation. I used to read all the documents that came with the pills. The scariest warning about possible side effects was on a bottle of a malaria drug called plaquenil sulfate: *WARNING: THIS DRUG MAY CAUSE CARDIOVASCULAR COLLAPSE.*

I wondered about the point of including that document with the pills. If my cardiovascular system collapsed, would I know it? And, what was I to do if it did?

AS is auto-immune system related. The biggest breakthroughs in recent years have resulted in some genetically engineered molecules like Etanercept (Enbrel), which suppress my immune system to keep it from attacking my moving parts. I know it works because I hurt much more if I miss giving myself an Enbrel injection. Obviously, it's dangerous to suppress your immune system, but it isn't that kind of drug that really scares me. It's the addiction to the pain killer that really concerns me. Methadone scares me more than all the other drugs I use.

I know that I'm addicted to it because I once cut my daily dose by 25 per cent just to see if I could do it. I never felt a craving for methadone. It wasn't at all like quitting cigarettes or needing Fentanyl, where the effect was mostly a powerful desire. Instead, when cutting methadone intake, I got physically sick. My experiment lasted just two weeks, and a physician experienced with methadone advised me never to cut my daily dosage by more than 10 percent. The truly terrifying possibility is that a methadone addiction can never be broken. Many pain specialists believe that you cannot get off of methadone, ever.

It took a long time to get on it, and the physical hurdles were similar to those I faced when trying to cut the dosage. The physical sickness was unbelievably powerful because, along with vomiting and intestinal pain, I experienced wild oscillations between periods of perspiring and shivering freezes. That went on all day and night, until I needed intravenous fluids to defend against dehydration.

Methadone does diminish pain. So does a non-steroidal anti-inflammatory drug (Celebrex) that I take in maximum recommended doses. There are additional prescription drugs on my daily schedule, but the pain level is still between severe to intolerable much of the time. It certainly is today, as I write these words. It was the same yesterday and the day before, and my supposition is that I am hurting so much because of stress. This manuscript has a deadline for submission, and it isn't very far away. It's painful to sit here and write, but it is painful to do almost anything most of the time. I have the motivation to write, so I write in pain because I've learned to do a lot while in pain.

I did a lot of performing on camera in pain. In my final decade of working, a device called a TENS unit was frequently connected to me through four electrodes. I had a pair of small knobs on a tiny control box mounted on my belt to regulate the Transcutaneous Electrical Nerve Stimulation intensity. The heavy tingling sensation produced by the device blocked pain messages and allowed me to perform without wincing, at least.

I was unable to turn my neck more than a few degrees at the end of my career, and the disease has always wanted to pull my head down until my chin touches my chest. The TV cameras were usually too elevated for my comfort.

I was forever asking studio camera operators to, "boom down', please." Some days, it was painful just to walk across the parking lot to go to work because any neck movement hurt, and it's not possible to walk without causing a little neck movement. Fatigue became a bigger problem as time went on, so I grabbed a short nap during my dinner break most days.

My roughest moment almost happened on camera. In 1996, at the GOP National Convention in San Diego, as New York Governor George Pataki walked away from my live interview with him, I collapsed. I was able to close the interview just seconds before I crumpled to the floor. It worried me because I knew that if I couldn't get up quickly somebody would call paramedics, and then I would lose time I didn't have before my next scheduled appearance on Albany's Late News. After standing still for a five-minute interview, my knees had buckled when I tried to move. I got up in time to avoid any special assistance or attention. Nothing showed on air -- at least, not in a big way.

In small ways, my condition intruded on my performances over the following seven and a half years. It happened more and more frequently. Pain caused even more fatigue than the disease. The newscast on which I found I could no longer satisfy my personal minimum standards was broadcast at 6 O'clock on February 1, 2003. It was a rainy Saturday -- a depressing, gray, and humid day on which the Space Shuttle Columbia had exploded. I really labored through my performance that evening and knew that was happening more frequently than ever before.

My evaluation of my on air work was never very good. I recall reading in David Halberstam's 1979 book, "The Powers That Be," that most network-level broadcast journalists did not enjoy watching themselves perform on air. I found that comforting. I never enjoyed watching myself and could always see big imperfections that other critics apparently missed. An odd movement of my right shoulder in stand-ups appeared very early in my career. Years before my move to WNYT in 1984, and before my disease was properly diagnosed, I had begun to notice a stiffness in my neck movements on air. On that dismal 2003 newscast after the shuttle exploded, the worst pain was from my swollen clavicle.

How does a bone like a clavicle become swollen? It turned out that muscle spasms in my back and neck were pulling my collar bone apart, and my body was adding bone trying to heal the rift. I went to my rheumatologist thinking that a cortisone shot would fix me up, but I didn't get one. Instead, I heard again that I was damaging my body with every newscast and that retirement was being mandated. It was time to try using pain medication, which I'd steadfastly rejected while working. Anything that reduced my ability to concentrate -- whether a drug, alcohol or even fatigue -- produced an unpleasant insecurity in me while performing on air.

Retirement helped me a lot, but my disease is progressive and, as one pain specialist told me, "The best you can hope for is status quo." The problem is that my current level of pain is hard to endure, and just getting older makes it harder and more painful. There are now four medical specialists who have advised me to try smoking marijuana for relief. I have, and it helps me sleep more than any other single drug. It also helps in a special way.

In my experience, pot makes it possible to overlook the pain by stimulating my ability to focus on something aside from the incessant hurting. It helps me cope, but it doesn't end the pain. Marijuana helps make music more absorbing, meditation easier and everything else a bit more distracting. Anything that can do that is helping me stay alive, at this point. Anyone who experiences this kind of pain and doesn't think of suicide isn't rational.

That's still unacceptable because of the effect it would have on my family. It does remain an option, though. On especially bad nights, when my whole being seems to tremble with pain, I think about escaping it through death. If methadone becomes unavailable, I would have no choice, apparently. The legalization of medical marijuana would ease some of my insecurity, but I have little expectation of that happening because I've lost almost all confidence in government.

And, I remain a reporter. That forces me to stay alive just to observe the world around me. I want to see how the story I've been covering for almost 70 years turns out.

If I can.

Chapter Eighteen: Commentators and the News

Two television commentators dominated my time in local broadcast television, and both became friends of mine.

Ned Pattison was a public official when I first met him. Our friendship began long before he first appeared at a television news studio desk with me. Alan Chartock was an established local media presence by the time I first met him. Chartock is quicker and funnier than Pattison was, but not as serious a thinker.

Ned Pattison was the most intelligent and dedicated legislator that I encountered in my entire career. I met him when he was Rensselaer County treasurer through a college classmate that he employed. Pattison was elected to Congress in 1974 after the Watergate debacle made it possible for a Democrat to win in what had been a solidly Republican district for more than a decade. Pattison beat incumbent Republican Carleton King, and that ended my effort to get film of a drunken area congressman.

When I first took over the assignment desk at WRGB in 1970, I began having a nearly daily telephone conversations with our reporter in Washington, DC. John Chambers was employed by General Electric Broadcasting to cover news in the Capitol for the company's three TV stations in Nashville, Denver and Schenectady. At the time, that meant Chambers regularly covered Albany area Representatives King, Samuel Stratton and Dan Button. King was the hardest to cover because he was not a hard working representative, and Chambers had encountered him in DC bars more than in the Capitol. On a few occasions, Chambers had cased King's favorite hangouts hoping to find him inebriated, but failed. The reporter assured me he would eventually succeed because King was known around the Capitol to be a serious drinker.

By the time of Pattison's race to oust King, I was a general assignment reporter for WRGB. I picked up a routine assignment obliquely tied to the congressional race one September morning in 1974. Admiral Hyman Rickover, the father of America's nuclear Navy, was holding a news conference at the Knolls atomic power laboratory in Niskayuna, which was run by General Electric. Congressmen King and Stratton would be present at the Rickover event, and I recalled other such meetings on what seemed to be a predictable schedule. So, on my way to the Knolls lab, I radioed the WRGB newsroom and asked for a check of the files for the dates of previous Rickover appearances.

They came every two years, just before the congressional elections. At the news conference, I listed the dates of his previous meetings to the admiral and suggested that the motivation for his trips to the atomic laboratory was political and transparent.

"Really," I recall Rickover saying angrily before failing to deny my supposition and trying instead to talk around my charge. I pressed him, and the admiral's anger grew until he finally shouted at me, "Listen, you are here because you have a boss who told you to be here. These gentlemen are my bosses," Rickover went on, gesturing toward King and Stratton, "and I'm here because they told me to be here."

The heated exchange played on all the stations as Rickover made my point for me. King and Stratton were angry, and Pattison thought I might have gone too far by insulting a national hero. At least, that's what I was told by an old friend from RPI, Owen Goldfarb, who was working for the Pattison campaign. The most interesting reaction to the confrontation at Knolls came months later from one of G.E.'s local press relations managers.

"You saved my job," he told me after the election. He explained that he'd refused the assignment to handle the Rickover news conference, and his bosses were very upset by his refusal. He'd told them, he said, that the whole thing was blatantly political and that reporters see through it and would savage GE if the company got too close to the event. It seems that his job might have been in jeopardy had I not confronted Rickover.

Pattison was one of dozens of freshmen Democratic representatives when the new 94th Congress convened that January. He immediately led a revolt against the seniority system, which had been in place in the U. S. Capitol for decades. There were so many new members, Pattison and others concluded, that their power within the Democratic party caucus was substantial. It was Pattison who suggested that they bind together and threaten to withhold votes for chairmanships unless House Speaker Carl Albert agreed to some of the changes the freshmen wanted.

Pattison's leadership abilities might ultimately have led him to become speaker of the house, some of his fellow representatives thought. I learned about that at Pattison's funeral in 1990 from Toby Moffett, who'd been a member of the freshman class with Pattison. Unfortunately, Pattison lost his bid for re-election in 1978 to Gerald Solomon, a dullard Republican from the New York State Assembly. It was one of many decisions by voters that reinforced my pessimism about the future of America. The biggest issue in the Pattison-Solomon election was the news of Pattison having confessed to "Playboy" magazine that he had tried marijuana.

My ethics forced me to avoid talking to Pattison throughout his campaign with Solomon. I knew we were friends and tried hard to keep my opinions from influencing WRGB's coverage of the race. Maybe I tried too hard. When it was over, my old friend Goldfarb called me and suggested I go back and look at the WRGB coverage. He felt that, in my effort to be fair, I'd gone too far and that the Channel 6 coverage had favored Solomon.

When I moved to WNYT in 1984, I brought Pattison on board as political commentator. I was always impressed by his extensive knowledge of politics and policy. I particularly remember his argument about the worth of a value-added tax. I opposed the idea (and still do) because all sales taxes are regressive, but I was impressed by Pattison's argument that the tax could be waived for exported items and thereby improve the nation's trade balance. Pattison brought a stunning depth of understanding to all issues.

One of my strongest memories of him is of the day he sat in my office and asked if I thought he looked a bit yellow. He'd noticed a yellowing of his skin while shaving that morning. He was right, and it was the result of a cancer that would kill him about 18 months later. My final meeting with him was at his West Sand Lake home, where we recorded a terrific interview. He was always far more optimistic about our civilization than me. Time, I think, has proven him wrong.

There's no question that Pattison, despite his intellect, was not a great television performer. The news director and I talked to him often about trying to energize his TV appearances. That's most definitely not a topic we ever raised with his successor, Dr. Alan Chartock. He was an established market television personality when he first sat on the WNYT news set.

His first comment – one that I vividly recall was said off air, right after he was seated – was, "I make more money than anyone here." Chartock probably was wrong on that. Nonetheless, he certainly was doing all right financially. He was a full professor at SUNY, the manager of WAMC public radio, an author and entrepreneur. He remains today a powerful personality of television and radio. We became and remain friends despite the fact that our daily appearance on television was almost always confrontational. It was a game.

Our only real strong disagreement on public policy was about capital punishment, and I think that he is not the strong believer in execution that he pretends to be. Sometimes, when people take a very public position on a controversial position, it is difficult to change it later without suffering some public ridicule by being labeled a flip-flopper. That may be Chartock's dilemma. He once asked me not to push him publicly on the issue because he had a problem in that whole area.

Most of our televised struggles over policy questions were staged. My job became to mount an opposition argument to whatever position Chartock took. Often, I could not successfully rebut his arguments, and I think he generally prevailed because I usually agreed with him. One memorable struggle was over educating the sexes separately. There had been a court ruling somewhere authorizing the establishment of all-boy or all-girl schools, which Chartock felt was wrong. He argued – correctly, in my opinion -- that the concept of "separate but equal" is always flawed because separate educations can't ever be actually equal. But in our discussion before the newscast began, a devilish plan occurred to me. Whatever reason for his position Chartock advanced, I countered with the mention that the building had separate men's and women's bathrooms.

When our discussion reached the air, I never mentioned the recognition by architects that nature required separate but equal accommodations for the sexes in toilet facilities. Chartock finally fell into the trap by anticipating that I would mention it and he did. I replied, "Why would I bring something so crude into a discussion like this?" He was left saying, "But, you did, ah, but…" before bursting into laughter after realizing he'd been set up. Our on air relationship looked contentious to some, but it was always fun.

The one exception was the time a minor scandal struck. A disgruntled former WAMC employee released out-takes from Chartock's weekly radio interview program with Governor Mario Cuomo that revealed that a clearly different relationship existed between the two men than what they displayed on air. I considered the tapes to be meaningless because reporters and politicians have always gotten close, but right wing radio commentators tried to make a big deal out of it, and I had to interview Chartock on the topic. Since he'd written a successful book entitled "Me and Mario," which detailed their relationship as friendly, the furor over the tapes which proved that it was indeed friendly was short lived.

However, the friendship ended in a squabble between the pair that demonstrated Cuomo's irrational sensitivity over mentions of his family. An April 1st quip to me on air by Chartock about Andrew Cuomo was reported to the former governor by someone who'd misunderstood it. It disappointed me that Mario Cuomo turned on Chartock so viciously based on something so meaningless.

Chapter Nineteen: Network Stars

Did you ever meet someone new and manage to utter precisely the perfect words every time you said anything? That's what happened to me with CBS anchor Dan Rather. The anchors from WRGB were in New York City to shoot promo motional announcements with him after the station dropped NBC and became an affiliate of CBS. I was the first to record, but Rather was late.

So, I sat at his anchor desk and waited. I first noticed the hairbrush and mirror atop a small table next to his chair. I was interested because I'd brought a mirror to the WRGB set and had taken some ribbing for doing it. It seemed to be a handy thing to have, and I ignored the kidding from other anchors and the floor crew. Then, somewhat out of breath, Rather showed up and took his seat next to me.

"Sorry to be late," Dan Rather said. "You can imagine what I was working on."

"Sure," I replied. "The Falklands. Or do you say Malvinas"

"I can't believe you said that," Rather replied. "I mean, you're absolutely right. If I say Falklands, I favor the British. If I say Malvinas, I favor the Argentines. It's amazing that you would bring that up. That's exactly what we were discussing. Did you see Chancellor's show last night?"

At the time, Great Britain and Argentina were warring over a small island chain in the South Atlantic that the English called the Falkland Islands but which Argentina knew as the Malvinas Islands. Rather's question referred to John Chancellor, who anchored NBC's evening newscast every weeknight and was Rather's primary competitor.

I told him that I hadn't seen the NBC newscast. He then started talking about Chancellor being too formal or stiff or something about his presentation that Rather found uncomfortable. I finally replied, "Well, I've always considered Chancellor to be sort of professorial."

"That's it," shouted Rather somewhat excitedly. "Professorial is exactly the word I've been looking for. Professorial. What a great word -- just great for him."

Before the morning ended, I was in Rather's office listening to him tell me stories. Ernie Tetrault and Liz Bishop were there as well, but Rather was talking almost exclusively to me. He was telling me that he knew that former U. S. Senate Majority Leader Howard Baker never ate breakfast, so that when Baker told Rather he was having breakfast one day at a national convention Rather knew he was lying. I told him that it was hard to comprehend that someone knowing the eating habits of a politician could get a story because of that knowledge.

When we left CBS, Tetrault wanted to bet me that I would get an offer from the network immediately because I'd hit it off so well with Dan Rather. I did not.

My encounters with other major network stars were never as warm as that session with Rather. On four or five occasions, I shot promotional pieces with Tom Brokaw of NBC. I never found him to be even politely conversational, much less warm. The first time I met him was on October 7, 1977. It was the 200th anniversary of the final Battle of Saratoga, and the sponsoring committee had asked me to be the Master of Ceremonies. Brokaw, who was then fronting NBC's *Today* show, had been paid $5,000 to travel to Saratoga County to read a speech.

He didn't write the speech. The writer the sponsors had hired to write the speech reneged on their deal, so I wrote the speech the night before the event. The sponsors were so appreciative that they paid me $200 for the effort and told me a story about Brokaw, who'd barely talked to me at all during the entire event. He hadn't talked to the people on the organizing committee much at all, and that had irked the woman who chaired the group.

On the car ride to the airport, Brokaw sat in the front passenger seat while the three committee members accompanying him sat in the back. Brokaw said nothing. He merely stared straight ahead in silence the entire time until the chairwoman finally said, "You know, Mr. Brokaw, you weren't our first choice as speaker today."

"What?" Brokaw replied as he wheeled around to look at her in the back of the car.

"Nothing," the chairwoman told me she'd replied. "I was just seeing if I could get you to acknowledge us at all."

She told me that Brokaw had said nothing in reply and just went back to staring out the front window. Do I believe her? Yes, I do, because I met the

NBC star on several occasions and never found him to be even politely warm. The last time was after he'd spoken to an Albany Business group at an area hotel. The WNYT anchors went there to shoot a quick promo for our news and for his network report, which followed ours. The promo never appeared on air. When I asked the WNYT general manager why the promo had never appeared he told me it was unusable. Why? Because Brokaw looked so unhappy to be there, and the producers couldn't cover him with other pictures. So, the whole effort produced precisely nothing for the station.

Tim Russert of NBC consistently went out of his way to help me, but I'd known him since he'd worked for Mario Cuomo in Albany. Both of us also were from the Buffalo area, and that helped the relationship. But Russert seemed inherently warmer than Brokaw. Indeed, every network star I ever encountered seemed inherently warmer than Brokaw.

Chapter Twenty: Telethons

I have no memory at all of how I came to be a host of WRGB's local portions of the Jerry Lewis Muscular Dystrophy telethon, but I performed those duties for more than 10 years. Those were marathon broadcasts that began at 9 O'clock in the evening and ran until 6 O'clock the following evening. We were on the air twice every hour begging for money and interviewing local celebrities.

I got to know most of the people connected to the local chapter of the Muscular Dystrophy Association as well as the victims of the disease that the association sought to help. Some, like Jerry Gravelle and his son, Mark, became close friends, but none were ever closer to me than the Cole family. Their son, John, was afflicted with Duchene Muscular Dystrophy, which was essentially a death sentence.

Johnny Cole was the poster child on my first telethon. He was there in his wheelchair every year. Eventually, I became friends with his whole family and visited their home several times. John's sister, Libby, still called me at WNYT decades later. My best friend in the family was Johnny. I got truly close to him as he grew up, and we did some funny things together on the later telethons.

One year, I tore his wheelchair apart to demonstrate how rickety it was. It was a maneuver to raise money for a new one. Johnny laughed and helped me. When he got to middle school, he made a candle holder for me in wood shop, which I still have. I always understood his prognosis. I knew that the damned disease would eventually attack his respiratory muscles and kill him, but that was initially 10 years away.

Then it was five years away. Then four, and then three and then two years away. Yet I still hoped for a miracle cure. Somehow, from my first telethon onward, I wanted to believe that the hundreds of thousands of dollars we raised each year would result in a cure in time to save Johnny. Then it was one year, and Johnny was still at the telethon, but he looked terribly pained and I could barely stand it.

He died at home, in his father's arms, at about age 13; right on schedule. I was devastated. I wanted to quit hosting the yearly telethons because some of my heart went out of it after Johnny died. Nonetheless, I continued hosting until I left WRGB. I had worked with half a dozen different co-hosts over the years. The last ones were Liz Bishop and Price Chopper supermarkets CEO Neil Golub. They continued the telethons after I left.

My basic reason for stumbling into a career in television news was that I wanted to effect changes that would make peoples' lives better. The most visible embodiment of that goal was my friend Johnny Cole, but I couldn't help him. But, when my grandson was recently diagnosed with a much less serious muscle disease, a physician specializing in muscle ailments told my son that a cure for Duchene Muscular Dystrophy is now close -- possibly only five years away. I was really happy to learn that. I hope it's true.

You can guess who I thought of first when I heard that -- my friend Johnny Cole.

Chapter Twenty-One: Norm Sebastian

We'd been friends almost from the day that Norm Sebastian started work at WNYT as the backup meteorologist. We worked together only occasionally, but we shared so many common interests that we became quite close over the decade we spent together at the station. Norm was also close to my wife, Donna, who listened to him discuss his relationships with various girlfriends endlessly. So, we spent a lot of time together and enjoyed many late night sessions just talking on my back porch.

So, it was natural that we would chat on the telephone on the night of October 2, 1987. He was in the hospital recovering from back surgery, and I was at the station, working. He told me that he'd had some weather charts brought over and had been studying them. He was amazed because it looked to him that Albany could have a snowstorm over the upcoming weekend -- a preposterous notion for the first week of October. That made me the witness to his prediction of a storm that became known as the October surprise. Nearly 20 inches fell and crippled the area for days. No other weather forecaster saw it coming.

When Norm was hired, meteorologist Herb Stevens, who'd worked with Sebastian at the Weather Channel, told me that the station had hired a "superstar" forecaster. Sebastian didn't like me giving him credit for his stunning prediction because he said he would never have had the courage to predict it on the air. But I knew him well and am positive that he would have found mentioning the possibility of the storm irresistible.

On his last day of life, a Friday, I'd taken the day off to go to his house in Averill Park to visit. He'd told me on Monday that his death was near, and he wanted to discuss life with me one final time. His kidney transplant two years earlier had caused physicians to suppress his immune system to prevent his body from rejecting the new organ, which had been donated by his sister. As a result, his body's defenses could not handle the cancer that struck his colon.

On that Friday, his sister phoned me early in the morning to call off my visit. Norm would not have recognized me, she said. He was drifting in and out of consciousness. That devastated me, but before I could tell Donna what was happening the telephone rang again. It was WNYT asking me to cancel my day off and come in to prepare an obituary for Norm. It was the most difficult assignment I ever had.

It meant screening hours of video tapes to find a few clips to sum up Norm's work. It meant writing a script to pull the clips together and to try to relate to viewers Norm's very special abilities. I cried a lot while working in my office all afternoon. By about 4:30, I'd finished writing my script, laid down my narrative and prepared cutting instructions for a tape editor to assemble the piece later, after the pressing news for the upcoming newscasts was finished. I headed home with great sadness, but I didn't make it. I was barely halfway across the parking lot when another friend of mine and Norm's, Eric Hoppel, called out to me.

He said, "Ed, come back. We have to edit the piece now. We need it now."

That was how Eric told me that Norm had died.

My obituary centered on Sebastian's obsessive interest in the weather and the wonderful sense of humor that he so often displayed on air. He was dancing in tights with Richard Simmons, using his necktie to demonstrate how the hands of a clock should be moved to accommodate the change to Daylight Saving Time and cavorting in a downpour that would have sent the rest of us scurrying inside. We finished editing the report just in time to make it on air. That evening, another news staffer, Jim Kambrich, went through still more file tapes and pulled a few additional excerpt that improved the piece.

Of all the newscasts we worked on together, the one I remember most is the one that caused a furor. On a Thanksgiving day, Norm and I worked because we were having the traditional meal at my house, and I lived very close to WNYT. It was a snowy day, and I heard Norm clearly state that, "there are six inches of new snow to the south of Albany and another six in the Catskills around the Town of Jewett." Immediately, the newsroom telephones started ringing. Callers were irate.

They swore they'd heard Norm say, "There are six inches of new snow to the south of Albany, and you can Jew it up another six in the Catskills." Perhaps a half dozen nasty callers refused to accept the fact that they had misunderstood Norm. We pulled the tape just to make certain, and Norm's narrative was quite clear. Nonetheless, callers savaged him as a racist and anti-Semite. He was devastated and hurt that any viewer would believe he would say such a thing. There was nothing we could do.

The staff put together a memorial service for Norm Sebastian. His sister thanked me for the obituary, and our lives went on. Norm was the second close friend to die of kidney fibrosis that year. The first, a former writer for the CBS Evening News named John Nelsen, also had spent hours on my back porch talking with me and Norm. They'd talked about their common ailment, but I had never considered it to be particularly threatening. Then, rather suddenly, they were both gone. They were really the first of my best friends to die. At least neither one of them had to go through the torturous experience of writing a close friend's obituary.

I wish I hadn't.

Chapter Twenty-Two: Election Night Coverage

The assassination of Robert F. Kennedy in June of 1968 shook American political life and brought profound changes to my personal life. My effort to cover the story caused me to be fired as a disc-jockey at Albany radio Station WPTR and sent me toward broadcast journalism.

By November, when the election RFK was trying to win was held and won by Richard Nixon, my focus was entirely on local elections. As news director at WOKO in Albany, I had just one assistant, Jack Aernecke, whom I'd hired a month before, and the two of us couldn't have compiled returns by ourselves. So, I enlisted the aid of the general manager, Jack Chapman, and a few salesmen. The result was that about a half dozen of us stole the vote totals from any station that had them.

We set up televisions in the station conference room and monitored the area TV news operations for election returns. It was a very significant night for the Albany County Democratic party, which lost state senate and assembly seats the party had controlled for generations. The Albany County Democrats also lost the district attorney's office, which had been in Democratic hands for decades. WOKO was too small to gather its own numbers, but we understood the significance of the results, and we turned it into a good night for the fledgling news department.

The following year, I was at WRGB-Channel Six and its sister radio station, WGY-810 AM. There I found the method of gathering election returns to be disappointing. Some reporters called politicians' headquarters and begged for results while others visited the county boards of election, copied down numbers coming in from polling places, then telephoned the newsroom to report them. It was messy, since it was impossible to know which precincts were included in the reported returns. The early evening results were sketchy and unreliable. Only when the election boards certified results near midnight could any contest be reliably called.

The same method was used again in 1970, and the result was unsatisfactory to the entire newsroom. There had to be a better way, and the rapid spread of computer technology provided it. The machines could tabulate the numbers from every precinct and keep running totals for every race on the ballot if we could get the raw data from every polling place. In 1971, WRGB/WGY enlisted the aid of veterans' organizations to collect polling place numbers. We used a General Electric mainframe computer to collate the data to generate fast and accurate returns for the first time ever in the Albany area. The mainframe computer displayed results on an primitive green phosphorus monitor, which was shot by a dedicated studio camera. The on-air result was a technological thing of beauty, but it was a broadcast journalism disaster.

The election displays were terrific, but the journalists had no experience with this type of continuously changing data and could rarely make sense of it. The on-screen displays were fine when viewed at home, but they were difficult to read on studio monitors, and the news broadcasters were unable to keep up with them. The displays were moving quickly, and most of the accompanying reportage was painful to hear.

Here's the sort of thing that the audience was treated to: "Okay, this is Rensselaer County Legislature …ahhh, Smith is leading … No, that's Jones, who has …ahhh, okay, that's gone, and we have Troy mayor now, ahhh, where … let me see … Ah, it looks like Abrams is … no, ahhh … Okay, that's gone, and we're looking at the county judge, I think. No, ahhh …This is state supreme court judge. Ahhh, I can't tell who's leading, ahhh …

The station tried to follow races in 12 area counties and assigned each of six studio reporters two counties to track. But there was no plan for the order in which contests would be considered, and the computer displays didn't include the first names of candidates. The system also required the reporters to do fast mental subtraction to decide which candidate was ahead. Some were better at doing that than others. Most reporters stumbled over names. A few of the in-studio journalists were reduced to senseless babbling for minutes on end. It was a simply dreadful television news product. Something had to be done, but how could election night results be scripted in advance?

By 1972, I was a full-time street reporter and handled almost all of the political news. I didn't want to see another rolling disaster on election night, so I decided to find a way to better organize the election coverage. It took a lot of thought and experimentation, but I finally found a way.

Every contested race got its own data page. Each data page had the same format so every reporter could find all the needed information about every candidate in the same place on every data page. That gave them candidates' first names and party affiliations at a glance. Above the names, I described the boundaries of the office being contested, since 1972 was the first election after the 1970 census had forced re-districting and most legislative district boundaries had changed.

Another data box described the candidates; their ages, jobs, affiliations and history. It was background information for ad-libs, as was the data box below. That one described the major issues in the race and, if it was possible, the expected winner. The idea was to help reporters identify upsets. But the key to my scripting system was the bottom box on the right side of the data page --- the out cue box. That was filled in only when the order of the on-air presentation was set. It told the reporter, the director, the audio technician and everyone in the building the exact words that would signal moving on to the next contest.

My idea was to give the working journalist all that was needed to ad-lib details of the individual race being considered and a way to end the consideration of that race and move on. It meant that I could lay out a five-minute cut-in or an hour-long report by deciding on an order for presentation of the races and then by pulling the needed race data pages and typing in an appropriate out cue. Often, the out cue was just another anchor's name.

So, an anchor might be facing a City of Albany block of races containing the mayor, common council president and one hotly contested aldermanic race. After describing the mayoral contest, the out cue box might read "SHOULD THE MAYOR BE UNABLE TO COMPLETE THE FULL TERM, THE COMMON COUNCIL PRESIDENT IS NEXT IN LINE." At the bottom of the common council data page, the out cue might be, "A LOT OF PEOPLE WERE WATCHING THE ARBOR HILL 4th DISTRICT COUNCIL RACE."

Whenever the anchor wanted to move on to the final race, the anchor could just read the out cue, and everyone in the building would know to turn the page to the data sheet for the fourth district. The bottom out cue on that might be simply: "ERNIE." Everyone knew to move onto the next block of races with a new anchor, Ernie, handling the contests.

It took me weeks of work, all at home, every year to write all the data pages, make multiple copies of them, then lay-out the order and type in the out cues. It worked just fine. A reporter had the information to fill a minute-long ad-lib if needed or the cue to move on after 10 seconds, if desired. My system even worked before the polls closed because there was information about each race to support an ad-lib about what was likely to be the big issue to voters. The polls closed at 9 O'clock in New York, and on-air coverage usually began with five-minute segments starting at 7 or 8 O'clock.

To fill those segments with some useful information, I decided to create an exit poll. I approached the RPI Department of Management Engineering with my idea to have students get the experience of interviewing people about their votes and then do the statistical mathematics to predict an outcome. I knew that WRGB couldn't pay a lot, but since the station bought beer and pizza for all the VFW and American Legion halls we could provide soda and pizza for the students in the Greene Building on the RPI campus. The department chairman liked the idea, except for the beer and soda payoff. He wanted something a bit different.

"Everywhere in the business world I go," Professor John Wilkinson told me, "business leaders tell me my kids are the best trained and brightest graduates there are. But, they spill ketchup on their ties and don't know how to handle a fork or make polite conversation. Your staffers are all experienced in handling public functions. Take my kids out to dinner with your reporters, let them see how to function in a social setting in suits and ties."

It was a deal. WRGB inaugurated an area exit poll with the stipulation that no race projections would be made before the polls closed. Still, demographic results could be given, and local results of statewide contests could be released early without affecting the election result.

The first year we used the exit poll, a mistake was made. The City of Troy was voting on a new city charter, and WGY predicted (accurately) the final result on its noon newscast on election day. We were embarrassed and rightfully criticized, but it was the last such mistake. I needed expert help in selecting polling places to sample. I got it from party leaders. The Democratic party chairman in Rensselaer County, Edward McDonough, and the GOP chairman in Albany County, Joe Frangella, were especially knowledgeable.

In 1984, Frangella found out how good the polling really was. In May, while I was still at WRGB, Frangella asked me to go to his house as a personal favor. There, he told me that he was considering a run for New York State Senate and wanted to know what I thought of his chances. I told him the truth. His chances of beating incumbent Howard Nolan in that 2-1 Democratic county were slim to none. Frangella got really angry and told me that WTEN's John McLoughlin had just told him he couldn't lose. He was really unhappy with my opinion, but he ran just the same.

When I left WRGB for WNYT, I took the exit poll with me. WRGB tried hard to keep the exit poll, and GM Jim Delmonico wrote RPI's new President, Daniel Berg, a fairly stern letter demanding that Berg intercede with his "underlings" in Management Engineering to keep the exit poll at WRGB. That was a huge mistake, as full professors at any university are not happy being viewed as underlings. The exit poll moved to WNYT, and one of the races we polled that year was Frangella vs. Nolan. My first election day call from Frangella was at about 5:30 PM. He wanted to know, off the record, how things looked for him.

I told him, "You're going to lose."

Frangella asked how big a sample we had. When I told him he bristled and called the result absurd. Of course, he lost.

The following year, he was backing a friend for county court and again called me at about 5:30 PM wanting to know how it looked. I told him that his friend would lose, and he again claimed that the poll, with its sample of only a few hundred voters, was ridiculous. His friend lost, and Frangella called me the day after the election and apologized. He went on at some length about how impressed he was with the predictions and promised never to doubt the exit polling again.

Eventually, Professor Wilkinson retired and the need to fill early cut-in diminished, so I eliminated the exit poll. Then fast computers and fast teleprompters made it possible to write scripts so quickly that the ad-lib data sheet method I'd developed was no longer needed.

That was terrific because there was an enormous amount of work involved in preparing those data pages and scripting out cues and sometimes much more. It always had been done by me at home, on my own time, usually deep into the night after I finished anchoring the 11 O'clock news. The thing that really bothered me was that after I left WRGB they assigned the election night producing chore to Bill Duffy. They gave him two full weeks off to work on it at home. That was more than enough time and, of course, he didn't have an exit poll to worry about, either.

Chapter Twenty-Three: Depth

No television viewer ever saw me encourage people to vote.

Throughout my career, I declined to participate in "get out the vote" campaigns after encountering CBS correspondent Eric Sevareid's objection to such drives just before I started reporting. He argued that such crusades were harmful to the republic. I believe him to be right.

There was no merit in encouraging people who were not sufficiently interested in public policy to vote simply because of their sense of civic responsibility. The popular slogan, "It doesn't matter how you vote, just vote," was and remains obvious nonsense. Of course, it matters how people vote . And, people who didn't pay attention to public issues and the debate surrounding them did the republic a favor by staying home on election day.

Station managers always accepted my view on that and never forced the issue. On other policies that I adopted their acquiescence was not so forthcoming. My resistance to news promotion in general, and especially to describing any TV news item as being "in depth," always caused me problems. To me, it was an issue of credibility, and my personal credibility was the underpinning of my whole career. All I really had that was worth anything was public faith in my integrity. It was my property. While television stations could rent it, they could never own it. My credibility was something I cherished and guarded. No news manager or consultant was authorized to corrupt it in any way. My style and appearance were involved in maintaining it as well, so while I would listen to suggestions about adjusting aspects of my technique I could not take orders to change it or anything else that I thought would effect my credibility.

From the very beginning of my career in broadcast journalism, I recognized the shallowness of TV newscasts. In many public appearances, I pointed to that and encouraged viewers to read newspapers or magazines to seek out depth. Many issues of extreme importance were far too complicated for broadcast news. Beyond publicly acknowledging that, I also sought out ways to assist in the public examination of complex issues.

I eventually became the Albany area's busiest moderator of high-level panel discussions. It was work that I enjoyed and therefore was good at doing. Some of the resulting symposiums were broadcast, but almost always on public television, where audiences were small. Many of the programs took place in academic settings, although I did a series of yearly discussions of economic issues for the New York State Business Council and other non-academic organizations. Over my career, I participated in over a hundred long- form examinations of complex public issues, usually without pay.

The most ambitious of my discussions were probably those which took place at Union College in the Nott Arena as part of a series organized by the Union Graduate Management College. Each year, the college brought in about a dozen experts of national prominence for high level discussions of complicated public policy issues. The deregulation of electricity generation and transmission was the first big topic they tackled. It took me over 100 of hours of study to prepare for each of the Union programs. I considered it necessary to become so familiar with the issues that I knew almost as much as any panel member. Sometimes, the resulting discussions drew national attention. After the electricity deregulation symposium, I received offers from groups across the country to moderate similar discussions in other cities, and I did moderate many discussions for electric power and business institutions.

I developed a style in which I used the introduction of each panel member to set-up the major issues. That made the order in which the panelists were introduced important, since as each was questioned by me for about 10 minutes to draw them out in their specific area of expertise. The most difficult of those set-up segments was in my panel on prescription drug costs. It was difficult because one panelist from Washington, D.C. missed his flight and failed to show up. That forced me to use other panelists to fill in the informational hole created by the absent expert.

All the Union college symposiums were taped by PBS local affiliate WMHT and then edited for time. My discussions commonly lasted three hours. A remarkably able director at WMHT named Dave Povaro edited them down to two-hour programs for broadcast. The broadcasts were generally repeated several times, so the exposure was broader than a single airing would get. As a result, I was asked to moderate many more discussions than I could manage. I handled complex discussions for SUNY-Albany, Hudson Valley Community College, Albany College of Pharmacy and my alma mater -- Rensselaer Polytechnic Institute.

The RPI discussion was an all-day affair to mark the installation of a new university president. The issues involved some fairly complex scientific factors, and I was pleased when a former RPI president, Richard G. Folsom, called me aside to congratulate me on the discussions at the end of the day. He'd headed the university during my undergraduate years at RPI, which were far from stellar, so his recognition was ironic, I thought.

In addition to those extended issue-oriented panels, I routinely hosted hour long PBS statewide broadcasts for the New York State Education Department. I came to know several state education commissioners on a personal level as a result. I found one, Rick Mills, to be exceptionally impressive. The years of work with him gave me a special understanding of the problems faced by public schools, I think. Those problems loomed larger and larger over the years, and I began to consider them insurmountable. Those programs played a role in convincing me to moderate my final seminars, which became the single most discouraging sessions of my life. The sponsor was NYSUT; the New York State United Teachers union.

Over the course of three days in October of 2007, I moderated a series of panel discussions for the union. The topic was the educational achievement gap that has opened in America. What I learned in the process plunged me into a state of near despair. The gap is in the educational results for children from poor families versus those from the middle and upper classes. It proved to be such a alarming discrepancy as to be obvious to even the dullest intellect that our society has a profound problem with its schools. Yet, most Americans seem unaware of it.

It means that about 15 percent of all American children will grow up so educationally impoverished as to be unemployable. The root cause is poverty, and it is self-perpetuating. Children from poor families are far more likely to have health problems for reasons ranging from exposure to leaded paint to asthma resulting from burning high sulfur fuel oil for heat. They're more likely to have been born underweight and to suffer early nutritional problems. They're more likely to have uncorrected vision difficulties, severe dental problems and even to have been exposed to far fewer new words in early childhood. They're much more likely to have been parked in front of televisions for major parts of their lives when compared to children from middle class families. They're more likely to not have a family, in fact, and to have come from single parent homes. Those causes are not related to school quality or curriculum, but the children of the poor are also more likely to encounter poor schools and deficient teachers as well.

The symposium took place three and a half years after I was forced to retire because of my progressive disease, and it quickly became physically challenging. Early on, I encountered a period of perspiration that became embarrassingly obvious. I'd missed doses of methadone, and the sweating was an early symptom of addiction withdrawal. At the time, my constant neck pain had started giving me morning headaches that were almost intolerable. By the third session, the constant hip and knee joint pain made it almost impossible for me to stand. I should have refused the offer to host the panels, but my awareness of the profound problem our society faces in public education almost forced me to participate.

My biggest problem was that the situation proved to be far more threatening than I'd imagined going in to the discussions. I'd seen poverty throughout my career and had reported on it many times in many ways. One report in particular, in the kitchen of an elderly poverty-stricken Albany woman, had especially troubled viewers. The unsanitary condition of the stove, the rotting TV dinners in her refrigerator and the insects and vermin with which the poor old woman lived had revolted viewers and drawn complaints from people who objected to having been confronted with my report.

The NYSUT discussions left me back where I started -- so profoundly discontented about our society's distribution of wealth and power that I concluded that the only honorable course was to work to change it. But my career is over, and my deteriorating physical condition seems to make meaningful work now impossible. So, my depression about our society now has the added weight of understanding that my work probably achieved nothing. A retiring RPI professor of philosophy asked me one day if I understood that we've failed

"Who failed what?" I asked

"Our generation failed to change society," he said, "and we knew we had to when we were young."

Yes. We did.

Chapter Twenty-Four: 21ˢᵗ Century Journalism

Several basic aspects of human nature make it almost impossible for anyone to sustain a career as an ethical and objective television journalist.

One is the desire on the part of most people to avoid hearing bad news. Another is an aversion to news that challenges established beliefs. Moreover, there exists the understandable reluctance to cooperate with any journalist whose work is likely to generate personal public disparagement of oneself or one's friends and loved ones.

Objective news reporting is as likely to deliver bad news as it is good. Objective journalism is as likely to challenge preconceived beliefs as it is to support them. News, by definition, is telling someone something that person didn't know before it was reported. Many people object to stories that can – and, in most cases, logically should -- alter their view of the way the world really works.

And, ethical reporting, by definition, pulls no punches because of personal relationships or sensibilities. It follows then that, over time, an ethical and objective journalist should generate many stories that will be found to be objectionable because of natural human temperament. Such a journalist is therefore unlikely to be popular. In television news, reporter popularity is all important to attract audience.

Television journalism is by nature particularly personal, since the final product is delivered on screen using not just spoken words but also facial expressions and gestures that necessarily convey emotional as well as factual information. The subtleties communicated -- intentionally or not -- in this personal presentation make the working television journalist more prominent than one working in print or even radio, I think.

All of journalism requires financial support, and all financial support stems from people consuming the journalist's work. That basic structural fact is at the heart of the problems that career reporters face. In newspapers, where circulation is the key factor in determining the fiscal health of the firm supporting the journalist's work, I think an individual reporter is assigned less direct responsibility for the rise or fall of readership. In television, where ratings are published almost quarterly, and where working journalists are more prominent in the public's consciousness, individual journalists bear great responsibility for an increase or decrease in the number of viewers. In major markets, TV newsrooms have far fewer working reporters than local newspapers have. Consequently, the market research consultants zero in on the television journalists when assigning accountability for the station's rating.

As a result, it seems to me that television journalists are subjected to greater pressure to give people news they want rather than news the journalist believes they need. In recent years, certainly on the national cable and satellite news providers, this has resulted in the selection of working journalists who espouse definite political philosophies. It also has clearly affected the selection of news stories covered and aired. So, objective journalists, those as likely to give fair and ethical treatment to both liberal and conservative viewpoints, are not as likely to be hired by those cable operations.

That also has been the case in local television markets where television journalists are evaluated by market researchers who assign 'Q' scores to reporters based, in part, on viewer's perceptions of how closely working reporters conform to the viewer's personal political biases. Those biases often tend to be regional.

For example, on the occasion of the opening of the Saratoga thoroughbred horse racing track, I once asked WNYT reporter Kumi Tucker on air whether she'd made any winning or losing wagers that day. Immediately, a newly hired assistant news-director from Alabama entered the studio to question the wisdom of my dialogue. He explained that in his former market I might have been suspended for asking about gambling by a reporter. In the so called "Bible Belt," casual references to things like gambling were off limits entirely.

On another occasion, a consulting firm sent a talent coach to Albany to work with WNYT's on air people. She'd arrived in town the night before our meeting and had watched the local newscasts. She told me that it took her some time to acclimate herself to the coverage she was seeing in Albany.

"Oh, my God," she'd thought to herself. "I'm in the Northeast where they still cover actual news."

She explained that she did most of her work on the west coast, where politics and government were rarely considered on local affiliate newscasts.

Another aspect of human nature I mentioned, the reluctance to cooperate with any reporter whose work has or might bring about unfavorable public opinions about a person or the person's friends and relatives, is certainly not peculiar to television journalism. But, once again, when the delivery of the finished product is televised, the reaction to the reporter is often more forceful than it would be if the story had been delivered through another medium. The result, across all of journalism, is the frequent coddling of sources by working reporters. That practice was highlighted in the case of the famous Watergate break-in story where the established *Washington Post* beat reporters at the White House and justice department complained that their sources were shutting them out because Bob Woodward and Carl Bernstein were writing stories that stimulated unfavorable public opinion about the beat reporters' sources or organizations.

In my own experience, I found some City of Albany sources shutting me out after I aired reports that were critical of Erastus Corning's tenure in office when details of his financial machinations came out after his death. I confronted one longtime source about that reaction and defended my reporting as accurate only to hear in response, "Yes, but the report shouldn't have come from you." Because the late mayor had given me more access than he'd given other working journalists, there was a belief by some that I had to be more supportive of his record in office.

In the 2010 case of the "Rolling Stone" article that ended General Stanley McChrystal's Afghanistan command, many journalists noted that it was written by a freelance reporter rather than a journalist working the military beat. The suspicion was that a journalist who wrote a story like that could not have been one who needed to maintain sources in the defense establishment.

At WRGB, there was a period when many of us in the newsroom, particularly co-anchor Ernie Tetrault and me, felt that reporter Bill Snyder's work in the state capitol had suddenly become very favorable toward Governor Hugh Carey. Tetrault speculated to me one evening during a commercial break that Snyder might be trying to land a job. The very next day, Snyder was named press aide to the governor. Had Snyder's reporting been more objective, the job might not have been offered to him.

Tetrault also identified the biggest failing of our local television operation with a marvelously insightful phrase. He adopted a slogan lifted from a commercial and applied it to our work as journalists:

"Time to make the doughnuts," he would say.

Tetrault used it almost every afternoon when he sat down to write copy stories for the upcoming newscast. He believed that the station management viewed the products of its reporters as the functional equivalent of doughnuts made by the Dunkin Donuts chain. Quality was less important than quantity.

Almost from the moment I started working in television news, I became resentful at the pallid degree of commitment to journalism made evident by management's conduct. Furthermore, as I talked to other reporters about the problem, I found it common throughout the business. I knew that enormous sums were being made on the news broadcasts, but the number of working journalists on staff remained shamefully low. One day at WRGB, I was asked to cover six separate stories for the one-hour newscast. I did it, but with full awareness that each one of the six was somehow flawed because of hurried filming, editing and writing.

At WNYT one summer, I began going into the station early in the morning to help select assignments for reporters. I stopped doing that after a while because there too frequently was only one reporter to assign. To be fair, both examples occurred during the summer months when vacations were being taken, but even on full staff days the number of working reporters was shamefully small.

The actual money being made on the news broadcasts was unknown to me until I left WRGB. When I did, my lawyer went to the station to attempt to resolve my status and left stunned. He told me that WRGB General Manager Jim Delmonico had said, "Ed might take three or four rating points with him, which is over a million dollars a year in revenue, and I can't let that happen." My attorney, Carl Engstrom, thought that Delmonico was engaging in hyperbole. I called WNYT manager Don Perry and learned that Delmonico had been accurate.

At the time, in the summer of 1984, Perry told me that each ratings point in a newscast was worth about $450,000 annually in revenue. WRGB's 6 O'clock newscast was then attracting 20 per cent of the area's viewers. A 20 rating meant that the revenue from that one newscast was at least nine million dollars a year. And, since it was a full hour of commercial content rather than a local newscast's usual 30 minutes, I suspect the actual take was nearly doubled. The

11 O'clock newscast had a 12 rating, which should have brought in another five million dollars annually. The station was paying me $40,000 a year, and I believe the entire newsroom budget was well under $2 million.

The actual income from advertising was dependent on demographic details within the rating reports. Sponsors felt that people over age 54 were no longer spending money on customary consumer items because their children were likely to have moved out of the house, leaving their parents behind to concentrate on saving for retirement. The real shoppers, sponsors generally believed, were viewers of age 25 to 54. News content was purposely skewed to attract those viewers. A market consultant once advised me to never write a story about viewers' Social Security payments, but rather to write about viewers *parents'* social security checks. The big advertising revenue went to stations watched by younger viewers. Stations whose newscasts were described as "skewing old" set commercial prices lower than those attracting younger audiences. Still, the stations could make a lot of money.

When President John F. Kennedy's FCC Commission chairman, Newton Minow, called television station licenses "licenses to print money," I had no idea how accurate his characterization was. When he described the content presented to viewers as a "vast wasteland" I didn't think he was referring to newscasts, but now I understand that he might have been.

The days of huge local news audiences are past, and no local television newscast in the Albany area -- or perhaps even in the entire country-- now draws a 20 rating. WNYT, in the May, 2010 Nielsen rating report, garnered the number one rating with just seven points. Clearly, tens of thousands of viewers have stopped watching any local television newscast.

That's partly the result of technological advances like cable and satellite TV and the Internet. I think, though, that it's also the result of local stations producing newscasts as cheaply as possible. For decades, I argued to managers that viewers were being driven away by boring newscast content and production. Some types of television news journalism, like investigative reports, legislative reporting or stories requiring substantial visual production, are expensive. Other content, known as "hard news" -- like house fires and auto crashes -- is cheap to cover. But house fires aren't very interesting to anyone except firemen and neighbors. Auto crashes are usually interesting only to the people involved and maybe to those whose commute was slowed by the crash. Neither has much real impact on the lives of viewers.

The cheap and easy news content usually requires less experienced and knowledgeable reporters than meaningful investigative, political or criminal trial reports. Courtroom news can be interesting and powerful, and it's often important for people to see, but it's also expensive and time consuming to compile. A TV reporter can cover six house fires in a day but just one courtroom trial. Auto accidents require no expertise to cover, but legislative or science news usually requires a journalist to have real intelligence and some depth of knowledge to produce accurate and interesting pieces. Almost anyone can collect interview clips (talking heads) in the state capitol corridors, but considerable intelligence is generally needed to identify inconsistencies and contradictions that can be the foundation for insightful and compelling stories.

Intelligent and knowledgeable people are usually expensive to hire. Good writers are in demand everywhere, and the supply is limited. Competence, experience, maturity and dependability are employee qualities desired by many enterprises that are generally willing to pay more than television stations. The "glamour of television," which used to attract bright and talented students to study journalism, has largely disappeared, it seems.

For over 30 years, I lectured SUNY-Albany journalism students on the topic of television news. In the mid 1990s, the head of the journalism program, Professor Bill Rainbolt, told me that he was contemplating a major change -- reinstating a textbook -- because he found his students increasingly unaware of world events and even recent history. Rainbolt had tried to open a discussion on the role of the press during the Vietnam War and found that the general response from students was, "What's Vietnam?" The best and brightest high school seniors were rarely considering a career in reporting news.

At that time, all of broadcasting was experiencing a shortage of male news anchors. Men were leaving the business of broadcasting. One basic cause was the enormous insecurity that had become routine for anchors. Men were reluctant to take jobs where their futures were dependent on focus group reaction to their receding hairlines and where the typical management response to a dismal rating report was to fire the anchors. Amazingly, one day in about 1980, WRGB General Manager Jim Delmonico berated me for risking my family's future by trying to maintain a career in such a "flimsy" business. He called me irresponsible for maintaining a career as a television journalist. I'm certain that it never crossed his mind that I might consider the job to be important.

Years later, at WNYT, the head of a consulting firm named Audience Research and Development, Ed Bewly, told me that I was too serious a person to be a news anchor. Bewly had started with one of the biggest media consultant firms, Frank Magid Associates, but had moved to Dallas, Texas and started his own firm. He'd been hired by WNYT before I moved to the station and seemed to be a favorite of one of the top managers at Viacom. Bewley and I clashed often over the content of WNYT's newscasts. Bewly wanted programs filled with undated feature stories, which he called "evergreens." He didn't believe that viewers wanted to see serious journalists covering current issues.

In my final, somewhat explosive session with him, I accused him of trying to push the station's newscasts toward becoming a version of "PM Magazine", a lightweight feature-filled magazine type program with several syndicated program blocks. I added that I would quit the business before becoming a "PM Magazine" anchor.

His firm's contract was not renewed, and eventually GM Don Perry hired Magid and selected Ron Turner from its group of advisors to work with WNYT. I liked Turner and had a good relationship with him. On the morning that I first proposed the "Live, Local, Late-breaking" format for a restructured 11 O'clock newscast to be named "Live at Eleven" it was Turner who was the first to endorse my ideas. They likely would have died on the spot if he'd opposed them.

Local television stations were almost always managed by people who rose through the sales forces. Perry had been sales manager before GM, as had his boss at Viacom come from sales. One reason the bosses needed advice from firms like Magid was their complete lack of experience in news. Station general managers were paid a share of station profits, so their goals were purely profit oriented. But television always was primarily an entertainment medium. News broadcasting was just a sideline -- a very profitable sideline -- but never the *Raison d'être* of the stations.

Television news operations were always too small to be able to cover town councils and school boards. Television followed the lead of newspapers and relied on them to find the news from the thousands of potential news-making events and groups. In the late 1960s, NBC correspondent Sander Vanocur coined the phrase "snippit news" to describe television news operations. He meant that TV news operations would snip the news article out of the newspaper and then film it for television. So, as the traditional news providers weaken under the competition from new sources enabled by technology, the most serious effect to our society is on newspapers.

No cadre of reporters stands ready to replace those being displaced by cutbacks occurring at newspapers worldwide. Fewer reporting observers are sent to monitor the work of planning boards, school boards, corporate boards or hundreds of other policy making boards throughout our society. News created by contentious decisions evaporates before it reaches the body politic. That necessarily raises the possibility of shock reverberating through society when the cumulative effect of unreported news becomes manifest. In some sectors, this potential for shocking development has been building for quite a while. Science news has been under-reported for decades, and emerging revisions of foundational beliefs may rock our culture when they appear suddenly full blown in a society given no earlier hints of likely breakthroughs.

Quantum physics stands poised to profoundly transform humanity's basic vision of reality and consciousness. Predictions of a technological singularity being created by computer science by 2030 are becoming more numerous and credible. Fermi's paradox might be resolved by stunning revelations for which civilization is wholly unprepared. Recent breakthroughs in genetic engineering may transform biology to give humans abilities once thought to be the sole province of gods.

Most people will have had no warning about any of this because journalists have shied away from covering science for most of my life. I heard lamentations about that from Cornell's Carl Sagan and RPI's Richard Fulsom. Now, I fear that cutbacks in coverage of all human endeavors are setting our society up for stunning news about events we could and should have foreseen had journalism not begun to collapse at the beginning of this century.

But, it has. Unbiased, accurate, edited and ethically prepared news is becoming harder to identify. People are inundated with information and unable to discriminate between that which is valuable and that which is worthless.

There's a problem that many people working in television recognized early on. It became clear that many viewers were not seeing the boundaries within the stuff coming out of the set that those us creating the stuff thought were clearly marked. Sometimes, it was amusing, as when WRGB's weather broadcaster Tim Welch's mother repeatedly asked him to give Johnny Carson her best. Carson hosted an entertainment program that followed the late news every weeknight. To Welch's mom, it made perfect sense that her son would see the man who followed him in the flow of stuff coming out of the box in her living room. After all, they were neighbors. The neighborhood existed in time but not space, but spatial displacements are invisible on TV.

In 1970, during my first year working in television, I already understood that the boundaries so clearly marked on my newscast producer's rundown were not discernable to many -- maybe even most -- viewers. That was at the core of my opposition to changing the practice of banning political commercials running within news programs. It was the first struggle that threatened my job, as it was made clear that if I carried through on my plan to appeal to the Federal Communications Commission I would be fired.

Advertisers appreciate the public's difficulty in distinguishing news content from commercials. Frequently, the makers of commercial messages attempt to disguise their productions as legitimate news pieces in a cynical effort to capitalize on viewer confusion. That's the reason I consistently refused all offers to front television commercials after I retired. There was easy money in large amounts available, but it was offered because I had retained my credibility through 40 years of public life. It had never been for sale because my concept of personal integrity would not allow that. Not then and, especially, not now.

Now is the most frightening time of my life. In our republic, where the people are sovereign, the sovereign is ill informed and yet inundated by a flood of information. We have no ability to separate fact from fiction as the institutions we created to help us do that wither in an economic system in which untruths can produce profits, albeit only in the short term. How can humanity overcome the fundamental aspects of its nature that work against learning the truth? I fear the answer may lie in learning the lesson that following our present course will create.

A very hard lesson that many, I know, will fail to learn.

Breinigsville, PA USA
22 November 2010

249803BV00002B/2/P